ACCELERATED LEARNING

in the classroom

Alistair Smith

Published by Network Educational Press Ltd
PO Box 635
Stafford
ST16 1BF
www.networkpress.co.uk
email: enquiries@networkpress.co.uk

First published 1996
First Reprint 1997
Second Reprint 1998
Third Reprint 1999
Fourth Reprint 2000
Fifth Reprint 2001
Sixth Reprint 2002
Seventh Reprint 2003

ISBN 1 85539 034 5

Series Editor – Professor Tim Brighouse
Edited by Sara Peach
Design by Neil Hawkins, NEP
Illustrations by Joe Rice & Oliver Shenton
Updated Memory Maps by Oliver Caviglioli & Ian Harris

Printed in Great Britain by
MPG Books Ltd, Bodmin, Cornwall

Acknowledgments

This book is the result of many years of fascination with the topic, fostered and encouraged by the inspiration and enthusiasm of colleagues.

The County of Avon TVEE 'Learning to Learn' project provided an opportunity to try out, test and refine the approach with staff from 16 schools. I enjoyed the enthusiasm and commitment of Avon teachers and I especially thank Chris Gray, Isobel Clark, Roger Gilbert, Anne Manuel and Chris Wardle for their contributions. Also Chris Lindop at Lawrence Weston for his consistent support.

Jim Johnston provided the original inspiration and support for this work. Rob Bailey and Barbara Teale were full of encouragement throughout.

In my research of the Accelerated Learning approach, it has become apparent that we all draw at the same well. This book utilizes and acknowledges many fundamental contributions. Accelerated Learning Systems material: Colin Rose and his book, *Accelerated Learning* and the Colin Rose and Louise Goll training pack, *Accelerate Your Learning*. Also, Gordon Dryden and Jeannette Vos, *The Learning Revolution*. Eric Jensen's books, *The Learning Brain*; *Brain Based Learning* and *SuperTeaching*. Howard Gardner's *Frames of Mind*, Launa Ellison's *Seeing with Magic Glasses* and Tony Buzan's *Use Your Perfect Memory*.

In sections of the book that deal with goal setting, positive reinforcement and use of language, I use material from Transactional Analysis and Neuro-Linguistic Programming. I received training in NLP at Practitioner and Master Practitioner levels from PACE Personal Development and International Teaching Seminars, London.

Sara Peach at Network Educational Press assiduously corrected my proofs and made many improvements.

Alistair Smith
April 1996

Accelerated Learning in the Classroom

The Accelerated Learning series attempts to pull together new and innovative thinking about learning. The titles in the series offer contemporary solutions to old problems. The series is held together by the accelerated learning model which, in turn, is underwritten by an informed theoretical understanding.

The term 'Accelerated Learning' can be misleading. The method is not for a specific group of learners, nor for a given age range, nor for a category of perceived ability. The method is not about doing the same things faster. It is not about fast tracking or about hot housing. It is a considered, generic approach to learning based on research drawn from disparate disciplines and tested with different age groups and different ability levels in very different circumstances. As such, it can be adapted and applied to very different challenges.

The books in the Accelerated Learning series build from the Accelerated Learning Cycle. The cycle starts by attending to the physical, environmental and social factors in learning. It proposes the worth of a positive and supportive learning environment. It then deliberately attempts to connect to, and build upon, prior knowledge and understanding while presenting an overview of the learning challenge to come. Participants set positive outcomes and define targets towards reaching those outcomes. Information is then presented in visual, auditory and kinesthetic modes and is reinforced through different forms of intelligent response. Frequent, structured opportunities to demonstrate understanding and to rehearse for recall are the concluding feature of the cycle.

'He would like to start from scratch. Where is scratch?'
Elias Canetti, *The Human Province* 1978

Scratch does not exist. At least not in the UK. I looked up my Road Atlas of the British Isles and could not find it. Don't look for scratch if you want to start afresh. If it has any sort of existence it is as a metaphor. To start from scratch is just not possible: literally or metaphorically. Why would it be desirable to start from scratch even if, a. it were possible and, b. you could find it? Might it be that the original experience was so pleasurable you seek to replicate it. Perhaps it brought with it an epiphany. Perhaps there were circumstances about scratch that you would wish to change. Whatever your motive you will struggle to start from scratch.

I wrote *Accelerated Learning in the Classroom* quickly in the summer of 1995. It was not then written from scratch. Others had used the term Accelerated Learning and described elements of the methodology. No one had, however, tried to apply what was an adult methodology to children in classrooms and write about the results. This was my scratch. I now know I cannot go back there again despite wanting to. I would like to start from scratch. If I was to write *Accelerated Learning in the Classroom* again, I'd do it differently.

'Hindsight is always 20-20?'
Billy Wilder, 1979

You may be familiar with the work of the educationalist Otto Hindsight. He and I have collaborated on series of perfect, if as yet unpublished, pieces which, should they ever reach the public, will change the face of learning as we know it. Hindsight is truly the greatest co-author and I commend all his works. If it was possible, I would start *Accelerated Learning in the Classroom* from scratch and work with hindsight.

When I read the book now, I think it has a great deal of practical ideas to offer, I think the Accelerated Learning Cycle is sound and the text alludes to a number of interesting questions which have since become the focus of critical attention here in the UK. I also think that the references to the brain and to human intelligence in the book have more metaphorical than literal worth and this is especially so for classroom teachers. In truth, brain research does not validate any learning approach, nor does it say that one 'must do this' and 'avoid doing this'. That is not the purpose behind research into the workings of the human brain. A by-product of research may be a speculation or a hypothesis relating to formal learning but it will not prove or disprove a learning theory. With hindsight I would change the interpretation of brain research in this book to be less conclusive and more open to question. To maintain that there is one gene, one synaptic connection, one chemical, one region of the brain or one hemisphere which is exclusively responsible for a given behaviour – whether it be related to learning or otherwise – is not supported by science.

For those of you who are intrigued by the references in *Accelerated Learning in the Classroom* to brain development and to the study of the human brain I recommend looking at *The Brain's Behind It*. This book, published by Network Educational Press in 2002, is an attempt to landmark some of the current thinking about the science of learning. Dissatisfaction with some aspects of *Accelerated Learning in the Classroom* prompted me to write it.

Accelerated Learning in the Classroom has become a text through which readers have been exposed to a whole new way of thinking about learning. The book directs its readers to other, and more challenging, works in this and related fields. It has acted as a primer for a more accessible and holistic way of thinking about learning. It has had an influence which was way beyond its author's original intent. It has forced its author into updating and revising his thinking again and again. In some respects it is now a piece of my own history and my own development.

There is a great deal of value in being able to approach everyday classroom challenges with a series of tools to hand. I think the Accelerated Learning Cycle remains a very powerful tool for structuring learning experiences. There is also some merit in retaining vestiges of the triune brain and left right ideas if only for the purposes of organizing classroom learning. In this way these ideas become metaphorical. Metaphors are also powerful tools when thinking about learning. Three further areas are also worth giving attention to.

Learning is all about seeking and securing connections. The connections phase of the Accelerated Learning Cycle is an opportunity to engage in such thinking. It is an opportunity to generate 'cognitive conflict', to pose those difficult – just out of reach questions – and to search for commonality of experience: what is this like? Where might we have met it before? What do we already know about this? What would be useful to know about?

The activation phase should be saturated with rich task-related language exchange. As a learner engages with a challenge, they are involved in generating a range of possible interpretations and meanings. The more we can provide opportunities for these to be exposed, shared and recorded within the experience and not after, the better. Feedback can be to or from oneself, another or a group, but it is best when it takes place within or close to the learning itself. Summative feedback drives out formative but it is formative which dramatically improves learning performance.

The review phase of the Accelerated Learning Cycle offers a chance for 'metacognition'. A chance to review process as well as content. Expose the learners to process and you give them more opportunity of becoming independent in attitude and approach. In the review phase, utilize a variety of methods – individual, pair, share and whole class. Structure the review phase so that you link to your connecting activities. Close with a preview of what's next. Thus we embed the cycle.

Finally a word about self-esteem. In *Accelerated Learning in the Classroom* we describe the BASIS model of building and maintaining the esteem of learners. In later work I refine this to include an additional element related to challenge. You cannot teach self-esteem. No end of affirmations, circle time or drawing customized heraldic shields in class will make enduring differences to a child's concept of him or her self without testing in real situations. Challenge is thus the vital missing ingredient to our esteem model. We then have the BASICS model of building and maintaining the esteem of learners. The whole debate around self-esteem is fraught with controversy. My view is that teachers can do three things and no more. You can esteem your learners, you can provide them with esteeming experiences and you can help them re-frame experiences and that's it!

Do enjoy *Accelerated Learning in the Classroom.* It was my first attempt to bring disparate elements which act on the learning experience together into a model which could be shared and explored. When I looked up my Road Atlas of the British Isles I could not find Scratch but I did find an End Point. It's somewhere in the Highlands and seems a really good place to start afresh.

Alistair Smith
August 2002

"The wise teacher does not ask you to enter the house of his wisdom. He leads you to the threshold of your own mind."
Kahlil Gibran

"Emblazon these words on your mind ... learning is more effective when it's fun."
Peter Kline

"To learn anything fast and effectively you have to see it, hear it and feel it."
Tony Stockwell

"The only kind of learning which significantly influences behaviour is self-discovered learning - truth that has been assimilated in experience."
Carl R. Rogers

so ...

"Whether you think you can, or whether you think you can't, you're probably right."
Henry Ford

"Whatever you would do or would wish to do, begin it ..."
Goethe

and remember ...

"Teachers affect eternity; no one knows where their influence stops."
Anon

Contents

INTRODUCTION

What is Accelerated Learning?

- ***new knowledge about the function of the brain in formal learning helps us to design more effective learning experiences***
- ***accelerated learning works with an understanding of unconscious as well as conscious learning***
- ***positive self-esteem and self-belief combined with the capacity to set personal learning goals underlies all effective learning***
- ***the Accelerated Learning Cycle builds in preview and review and adopts Howard Gardner's model of multiple intelligences***
- ***the principles of accelerated learning are summarized by the acronym: NO LIMIT***

Accelerated learning is an umbrella term for a series of practical approaches to learning which benefit from new knowledge about how the brain functions; motivation and self-belief; accessing different sorts of intelligence; and retaining and recalling information. Accelerated Learning carries with it the expectation that, when properly motivated and appropriately taught, all learners can reach a level of achievement which currently may seem beyond them. The Accelerated Learning approach will help students understand their own learning preferences better. It will impart lifelong skills in the processes of learning. Students will learn to learn.

What accelerated learning offers is a structured system in which this new knowledge about the learner, learning and the learning environment comes together. Much of it is in everyday evidence in classrooms without having a tag attached to it or without all the elements or the sequence I describe. The best classroom practice does not assume that teaching and learning necessarily co-exist; it starts from the needs of the learner; it is differentiated and motivational and is fun, lively and engaging. As such it is accelerative because it allows the learner to fulfil his or her potential.

How to use this book ...

- ***be clear what your purpose is in reading the book***
- ***skim the book first to get a sense of its layout***
- ***read the bullet points heading each chapter***
- ***look at each summary memory map***
- ***select your key areas of interest***
- ***read each opening section***
- ***build up notes using appropriate techniques***
- ***review using key questions***
- ***ask yourself how you can apply the new knowledge***

The principles of Accelerated Learning can be summarized in the acronym: NO LIMIT

kNow

The first principle is to k**N**ow the brain and how it works in formal learning situations. An understanding of the three parts of the brain – the reptilian, limbic and neo-cortex - and what functions they control will help teachers to design appropriate learning environments which are challenging, without being stressful, and which deliver whole-brain, holistic learning. Lesson structure and content which demonstrates awareness of the different needs of right and left brain learners will automatically have a greater impact.

Open

When we **O**pen and relax we are more receptive to new information and ideas. The optimum condition for learning is a state of relaxed alertness. The learner feels supported and confident that risks can be taken. Learning is fun and non-threatening. Links between the new experience and the personal goals of the learner are easily made. By knowing where he or she is in relation to work completed and work to come, and by being open and relaxed about it, success is more likely. We can utilize music to help access this exact state for our learners.

Learning

Learning to capacity requires the teacher to provide a challenging but supportive environment where learning operates at a number of levels. The learner is encouraged to set very high personal goals and to identify specific targets to help in working towards them. Teacher expectations are passed on consciously and unconsciously, so it becomes important to affirm the successes of the learner.

Input

Effective teaching will **I**nput through visual, auditory and kinesthetic means (VAK). Also, Neuro-Linguistic Programme (NLP) work has successfully demonstrated that communication between two persons takes place in the dominant or preferred representational systems. A classroom of learners will include 29 per cent who are visual learners, 34 per cent who are auditory learners and 37 per cent who are kinesthetic learners. To avoid teaching in our own preferred system most or all of the time we need to have a repertoire of strategies. Without this our communication is largely with one group.

Multiple

In addition to the use of VAK in our repertoire we need to add specific strategies which can be utilized to access the **M**ultiple intelligences. We can identify the individual balance of intelligences in the learners in our classroom and manage our teaching accordingly. In many ways the extent to which one agrees with Gardner's theory of multiple intelligence is irrelevant. What it offers is a schema whereby we can provide a variety of teaching and learning strategies to accord with the differing ways in which our students learn.

By building and maintaining self-belief and self-esteem in the learner we **I**nvest more. We can best achieve this by providing a learning environment which generates a sense of belonging; encourages and helps fulfil aspirations; is safe; helps to acquire a sense of identity; and provides opportunities for success.

Invest

In such an environment students are encouraged to **Try** it, test it and review it. Try out and explore the new learning methods and find out which are successful. Put them to the test by explaining or demonstrating new skills and knowledge to others and constantly reviewing using the different methods described in this book.

Try

NO LIMIT

- k**N**ow the brain and how it works
- **O**penness and relaxation for optimum learning
- **L**earn to capacity
- **I**nput through VAK – Visual, Auditory and Kinesthetic
- **M**ultiple intelligence activities
- **I**nvest more through BASIS
- **T**ry it, test it and review it

The Accelerated Learning Cycle

The Accelerated Learning Cycle (described in full in Sections Three and Seven) has seven stages. Each stage and its place in the cycle is of equal importance. A further pre-stage – the supportive learning environment – is a constant, and operates like a guide-rail keeping the Accelerated Learning Cycle running true.

In this book the relevance of each section to the Accelerated Learning Cycle is shown by a graphic next to the heading.

The Accelerated Learning Cycle looks like this ...

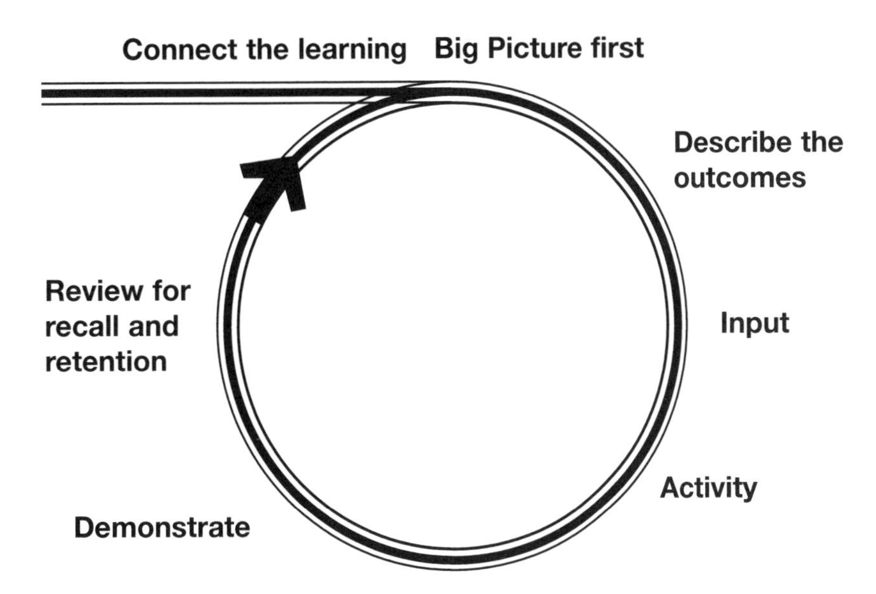

Memory Map of the contents of Accelerated Learning

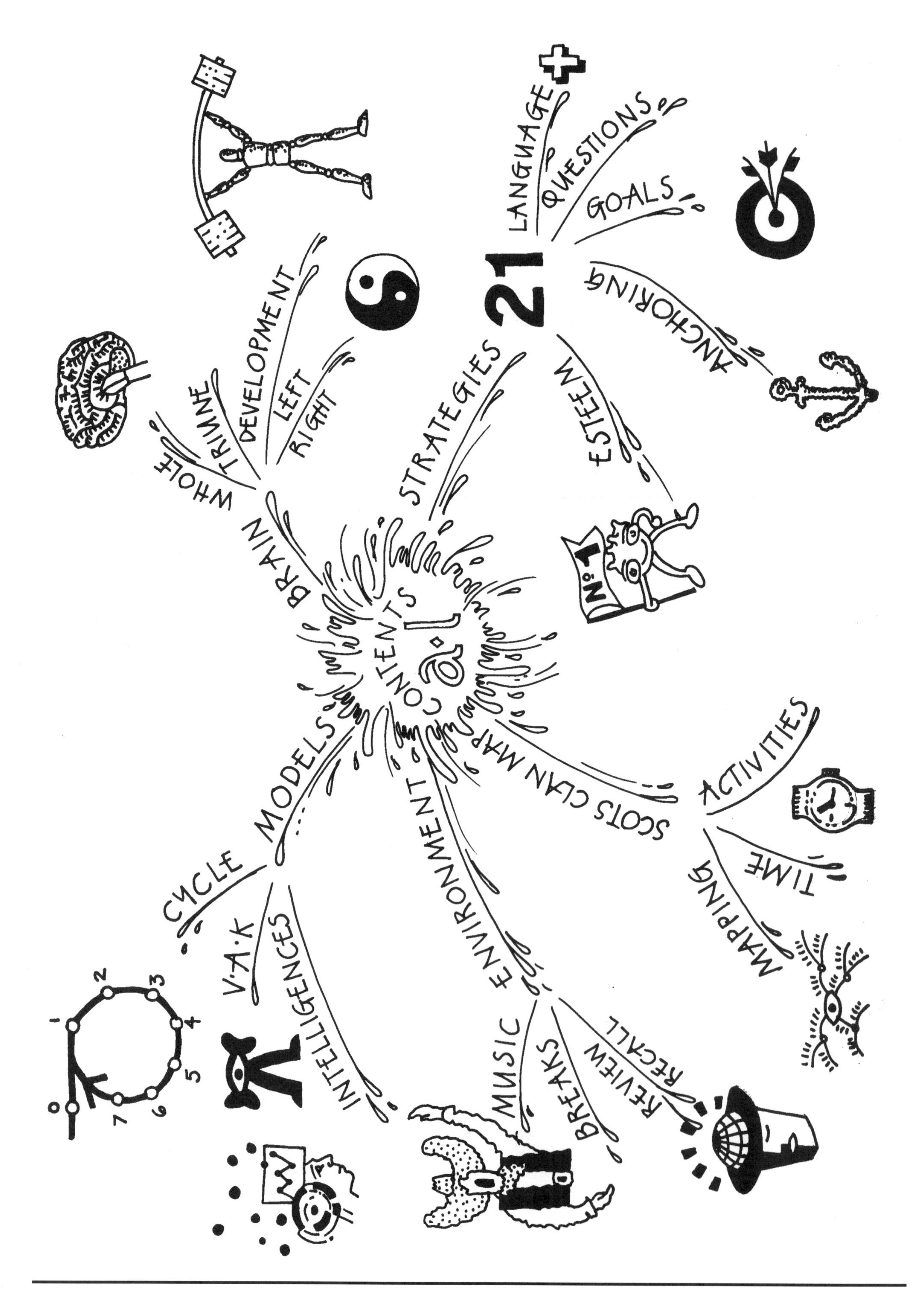

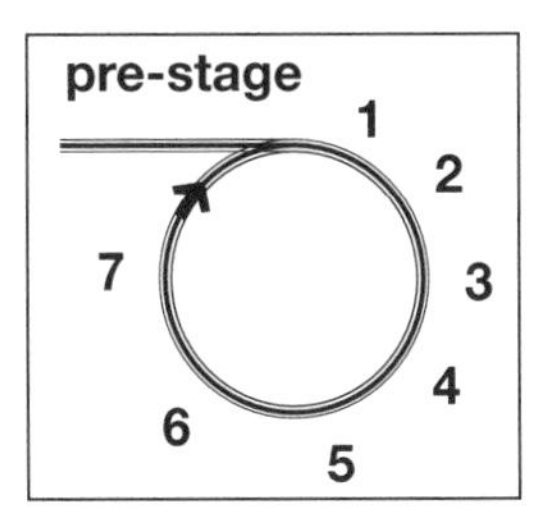

The brain in learning

In Section One you will learn how ...

- *80 per cent of knowledge about the functions of the brain in learning has emerged in the last 20 years*
- *the brain is designed for survival not formal learning*
- *an understanding of how the brain functions helps us to improve the design of learning experiences*
- *a state of relaxed alertness – high challenge and low stress – is best for learning*
- *the three parts of the brain all perform different specialist functions in learning*
- *accelerated learning connects both left and right brain and utilizes underused capacity*

In the last 20 years 80 per cent of our knowledge about the brain and how it learns has been accumulated. Understanding about the different functions of specific parts of the brain has led to a more sophisticated appreciation of what happens to the brain in learning situations. However, this new knowledge is, for the moment, playing little or no part in influencing the design of the experiences we provide for students in our classrooms. Indeed, much of what happens in classrooms throughout the country conflicts with what is now known about the brain and its design.

The Brain in Learning

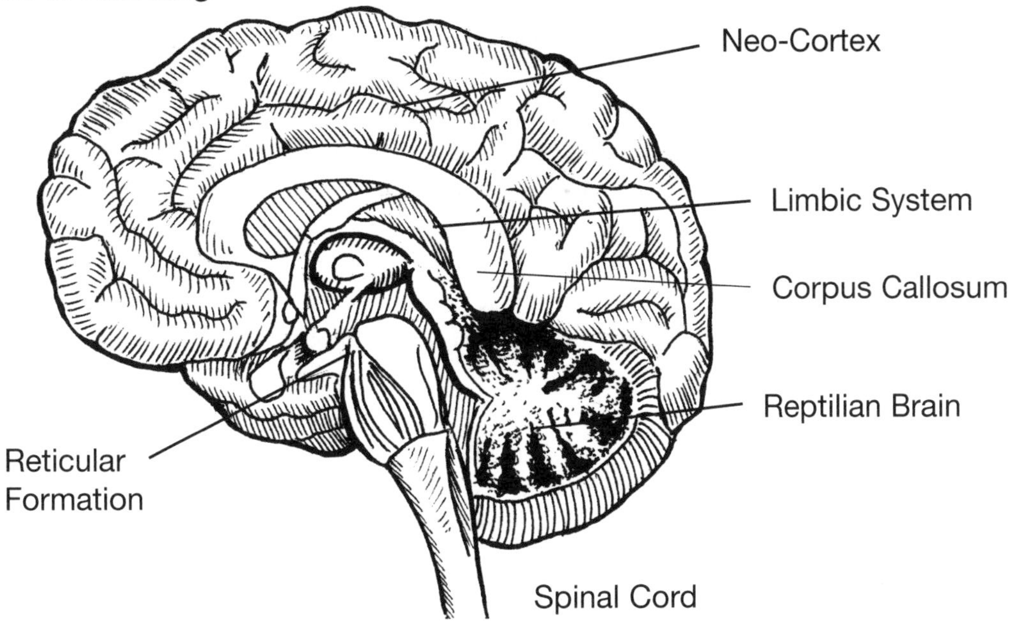

The brain is designed for survival. This is most important when considering the design of learning experiences. Under stress or anxiety the brain prioritizes its survival function and downloads in order to secure survival behaviours. The brain is also designed to process data as a whole rather than in parts; holistically rather than discretely.
It develops best when processing many inputs at once and at many different levels of consciousness. This means that effective learning environments should be multi sensory and holistic. They should also be personalized; attuned to the self-interest of the learner and to the development stage of the brain.

Development of the brain

There are biological determinants to the thinking capacities of young adults. An understanding of these biological determinants, particularly the development of the brain, helps in recognizing what can reasonably be expected in terms of problem solving and reasoning powers at different ages. We now know that the stages of development which the pioneering educational theorist Jean Piaget described, correspond to the biological stages of brain development.

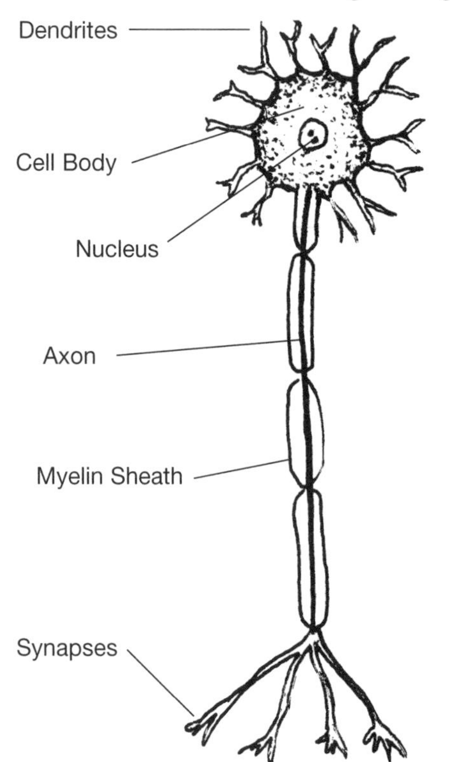

The building block within the brain upon which all thinking is based is the neuron. A neuron contains a cell, axons and dendrites. There are about one hundred billion neurons, or nerve cells, in the brain. Each is capable of making connections with any of the others. This is when learning takes place. Robert Ornstein has said that, 'In a single human brain the number of possible interactions between cells is greater than the number of atoms in the known universe.' Our expectations of learners and of our own capacity for learning is consistently too low. It can contribute to a self-fulfilling prophecy of low achievement and apathy. To avoid this trap we need to constantly remind ourselves of the brain's capacity for learning.

A neuron is a self-contained communication centre with an information sending facility and an information receiving facility. The sending facility at one end of the neuron comprises axons and the receiving end comprises dendrites. These are like tiny fronds which seek to connect with other fronds. Cells communicate with each other electrically and then chemically. Repeated stimulation causes sender and receiver to route closer together in an electrical jump or synapse. The more frequent the stimulation the more permanent the connection. This is the biological equivalent of learning. These neuron pathways are laid down as we grow older and the connections between experiences are made. The more the connections are made, the more permanent and well-established the pathway and the easier it is for further learning to take place. Like many pathways some are well-used while others are neglected. When, after years of neglect, you return to an overgrown path it is very easy to restore it to its original state. When you think you've forgotten an experience you learned when younger, it often comes back very quickly. The connections are already in place.

A new learning experience needs to be located on, or connected to, existing pathways for meaning to be generated. For this to happen there must be appropriate sensory stimulation. If a young learner does not have the experience with which to connect information, then no learning takes place. Neurons must connect with other neurons for meaning to be created. This is why learning is related to the development stage of the child. Brain development in a child can be as much as 20 months in difference to chronological age. Plateaux and spurts in brain growth are a normal part of development.

Estimates vary about how much of our brain capacity we use. From as little as 2 per cent to 25 per cent at most. The implications for individualising learning begin to become apparent as our understanding of the brain in learning improves.

As the brain develops, the process of myelination takes place. Myelination is the sheathing of the neuron's transmitting end – the axon – in a chemical coat. Myelination improves the effectiveness of connections between cells. It puts a permanent surface on the pathway where before there may have only been the tread of many journeys. It takes place in different parts of the brain as a child grows and develops, with the prefrontal lobe – the area of cognitive operation – the last to develop at about 16 years of age.

The stages of brain development align roughly with Piaget's observed stages of child development and caution us as teachers and educators that we ought not to expect youngsters to function as small adults or with a capability which is biologically out of reach. Learning experiences which are insufficiently developmental and are not stimulating, bore the youngster, whereas activities which are beyond their capacity given their developmental stage are confusing. The young learner's capacity to handle data and problem solving requires sufficient pathways to be in place. For the pathways to be in place requires a plethora of experiences and understanding and interpretation of those experiences which is not always to hand.

The best way to encourage the maturation of the myelination process is to encourage higher order thinking skills for the development stage and to rehearse these skills in a wide variety of contexts. Interpretation of data becomes more important than accumulation of data; opinions and viewpoints more important than knowledge of facts. The work of Reuven Feuerstein on instrumental enrichment and cognitive modifiability has pioneered this field. In this country the Cognitive Advancement in Science (CASE) and Cognitive Advance in Maths (CAME) projects and the Somerset Thinking Skills project have recorded notable successes and would reward further investigation by the reader.

The triune brain

The work of Dr Paul MacLean of the United States Institute of Mental Health firmly established that the brain has three distinct parts whose separate but related functions are active in any learning experience. An understanding about these functions assists in our teaching.

The three parts of the brain are the reptilian brain, the mid-brain or limbic system and the neo-cortex. A good way of understanding how they position together is to take your right hand and form a fist. Place your left palm on top and wrap it around. The right wrist is like the reptilian brain coming up from the spinal cord. The fist is like the limbic brain sitting on top and the left hand like the neo-cortex wrapping itself around the limbic brain.

The reptilian brain

The reptilian brain includes the brain stem, pons, pyramid and cerebellum. Between the well-defined nuclei and tracts, the brain stem consists of more diffusely arranged nervous tissue, the reticular formation (RAS). At the top end of the spinal cord, the reptilian brain is sited in the opening in the bottom of the skull, and is the part of the brain responsible for:

- **survival** – fight or flight responses; lashing out; screams.
- **monitoring** motor functions – breathing; balance; and instinctual responses.
- **territoriality** – defensiveness about possessions; friendships; personal space.
- **mating rituals** – attention seeking; showing off.
- **hierarchies** – the need to be, or be associated with, the gang leader.
- **rote behaviours** – behaviours which are repetitive, predictable and rarely constructive.

This part of the brain is the oldest and is configured for survival. Under negative stress the reptilian brain dominates. The functions described above lock into place. This is a key fact for teachers.

Some causes of learner stress:
- ***disputes with parents, friends or teachers***
- ***victimization, bullying, cliques,gangs, personal threats, low self-esteem, lack of self-belief, negative self-talk***
- ***inability to connect learning with personal goals or values***
- ***belief that the work is too difficult; inability to make a beginning on tasks***
- ***inability to understand the connections between current and past or possible future learning***
- ***physical or intellectual difficulty in accessing material as presented***
- ***poor sight or hearing***
- ***distractions in the learning environment***
- ***poor self-management and study skills***

The use of Computerized Axial Tomography (CAT) scans and Magnetic Resonance Imaging (MRI) has allowed neurologists to demonstrate the effect of different cognitive activity on the brain under stress. Blood flows towards the reptilian brain and away from the higher order processing functions in the other parts of the brain. Chemicals such as adrenaline, catecholamines and cortisol are injected into the bloodstream to ensure a quick response. The heart rate increases. Blood vessels are constricted in the skin and intestines and blood leaves these areas. The blood pressure rises and the increased supply of blood is made available to the reptilian brain. This closing down effect under perceived threat results in the control functions listed above displacing the capacity for patterning, problem solving, creativity, flexibility and peripheral awareness. Higher order thinking skills are displaced by survival, ritualistic and rote behaviours. An individual loses peripheral vision, focusing on the source of anxiety, resorting to behaviours learned in early childhood.

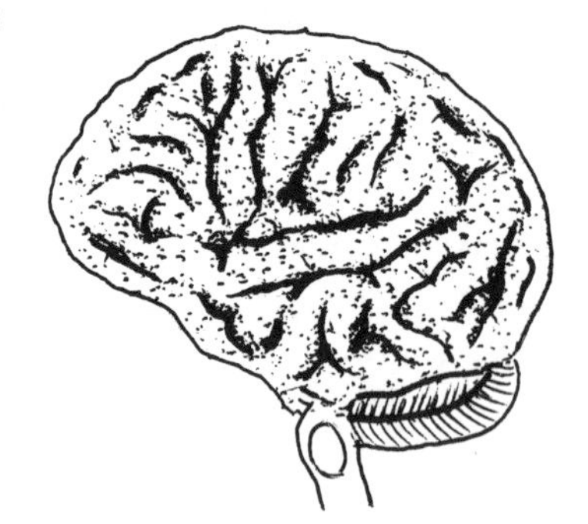

Scan of brain in normal activity

This means that the learner under stress will resort to rote and ritualistic responses, fight or flight responses and be resistant to innovation or new information. A learner in your classroom who is under stress or anxiety will not learn anything! It is biologically impossible!

Learner stress can emerge from a number of circumstances: as a result of physical or emotional threat, a lack of self-purpose, an inability to form relationships with peers or a sense of isolation. Difficulties with intellectual understanding perhaps exacerbated by constraints of time or resource in academic work would also induce learner stress. To help overcome some of these difficulties the teacher can develop teaching practices and supportive classroom rituals which reduce learner stress. Examples of how this can be done are summarized here and dealt with in detail in later sections.

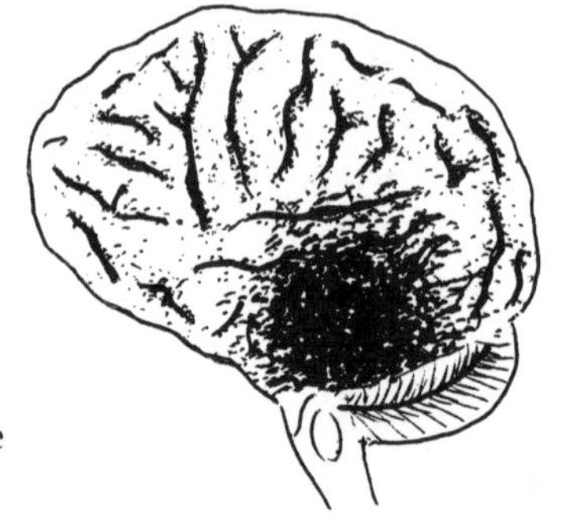

Scan of brain under stress (showing closing down effect)

☞ *Relaxation techniques*. By practising relaxation techniques and familiarizing your class with them, you not only help students get into the right state for learning, you also exercise a powerful classroom management tool. Help them to practise breathing by sitting upright with feet firmly planted on the floor. Breath gently and smoothly following the breath from the stomach, expanding into the lungs and then up through the throat. Eyes closed, ask them to visualize their breath following this journey each time. In addition, you can help them understand the difference between a tense and stressed state and a relaxed one by working down the body tensing and relaxing the head, the face, the neck and the shoulders down to the toes.

☞ ***Early team building.*** Activities which are inclusive rather than exclusive help learners lose the stress that comes with inhibition. Good examples are those which require students to find out then share positive things about others in the class. The teacher can very easily assemble a set of questions which will prompt this dialogue. The outcomes can be displayed on a class collage. A refinement is to devise a series of statements which describe a positive quality or experience unique to one member of the class. Write all of these onto a card. Each member of the class then has to collect an autograph for each statement on the card. Team activities can and ought to be developed with the class as their academic year progresses.

☞ ***Rituals or routines around the beginning and ending of lessons.*** You should develop familiar opening and closing rituals which anticipate the learning experience to come. Montessori teachers are trained to welcome every child personally at the start of lessons. Simply standing by the door, smiling and making eye contact helps!

☞ ***Consistent expectations***. For many of your students, school and their everyday experiences will be the only occasion in their lives where they can guarantee a level of certainty in how they will be treated. This consistency is vital and to work to best effect must be applied throughout the school. A negotiated and agreed behaviour policy based on building and maintaining positive self-esteem, widely understood and consistently applied and reinforced through positive teacher expectations and behaviour, will do more than anything else to accelerate learning. Avoid artificial deadlines, empty threats and group sanctions.

☞ ***Building and maintaining learner self-esteem.*** Wherever possible provide positive and regular feedback at a formal and informal level. Focus on past successes however small. Use these to build visions of future successes. Help learners set appropriate learning goals for themselves and review these regularly.

The limbic system

The second part of the brain is the middle-brain. The middle-brain or limbic system controls the emotions, maintenance functions and, most significantly, is the site of long-term memory. The limbic brain is a system of seven areas which includes the hypothalamus and hippocampus, the pituitary, the reticular system and the thalamus. This part of the brain runs our emotions and our immune system, dictates sleeping cycles, eating patterns and sexuality. It also, through the reticular system, which sits at the top of the reptilian brain, routes information to where it is needed.

The reticular system filters in useful and valued information and filters out useless information. This is the part of the brain which validates new knowledge and, as such, is sited in the area of the brain associated with the long-term memory and emotions. For the brain to validate learning there must be an emotional connection. The learning must be associated with a purpose which the learner has set. Strong, personal and real learning goals are therefore imperative for accelerated learning.

There are more neural pathways extending up into the higher cognitive part of the brain than there are coming back. This means that the limbic system is pre-eminent in processing and managing information. The brain values emotions and emotional associations more than higher order thinking skills. This is important in understanding memory and particularly in siting new knowledge in the long-term memory.

The limbic area thus holds all three parts of the brain in balance and links long-term memory with emotion.

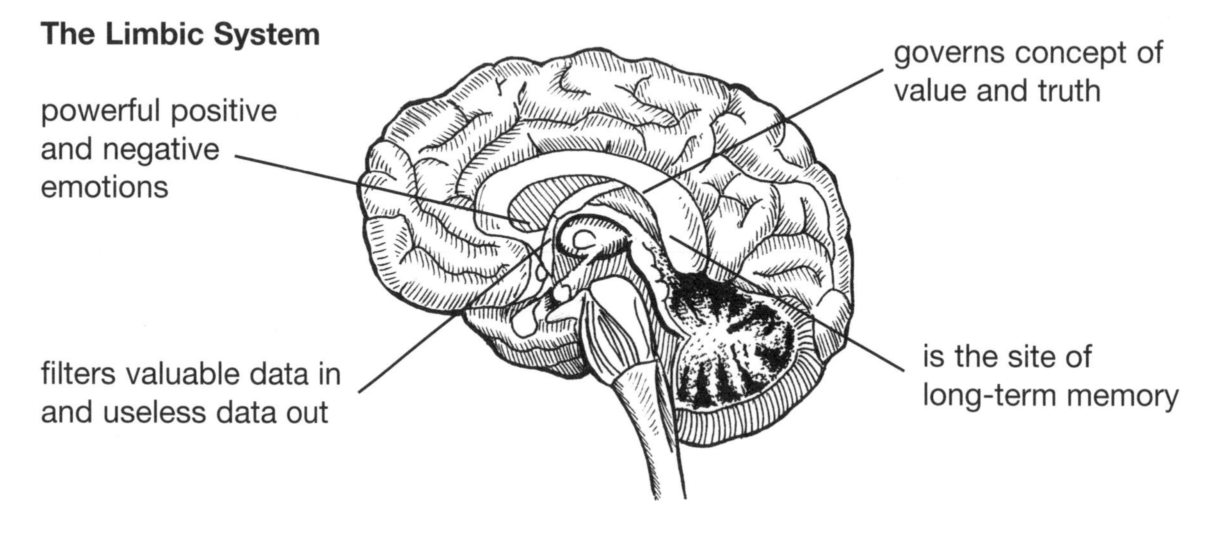

There are three key points for learning here. Firstly, emotions and emotional associations are more important to the brain than cognitive understanding.

Secondly, the limbic brain governs our concept of value and truth – although we may reason that information is true, it is only when it is linked with feelings via the limbic system that we assign it value. It is also the part of the brain that governs goal-setting. Goals which have a powerful personal link connect with emotions and activate the reticular system to filter valuable and relevant data in, useless data out.

Thirdly, information with a powerful attachment to emotions or feelings will reside in the long-term memory. An experience which has a strong emotional association will be easier to remember. Emotional associations can be generated in the design of the learning experience.

The neo-cortex

The cerebrum or neo-cortex is the 'thinking cap'. The neo-cortex looks like a folded newspaper crumpled up and sitting on top of the mid-brain. Unfolded and flattened out, the cerebrum would occupy several square metres. It is divided into four lobes and separated into two halves – the left and right hemispheres. The two hemispheres are joined by the corpus callosum. The corpus callosum acts like a central telephone exchange relaying messages between left and right hemispheres. The corpus callosum is larger in women's brains.

The neo-cortex is the part of the brain which has evolved most recently. It is the part of the brain used in problem solving, discerning relationships and patterns of meaning. The brain seeks to generate meaning from the sensory data which it is presented with. It does so at all times. Research at Bell Laboratories found that even when we come up with an appropriate solution to a problem, the brain continues processing for alternative and additional solutions non-consciously.

This pattern-making function of the neo-cortex is crucial. Eric Jensen, in his book, *Brain-Based Learning and Teaching,* makes some very good points about holistic, multi-path learning. 'Any group instruction that has been tightly, logically planned will have been wrongly planned for most of the group, and will inevitably inhibit, prevent, or distort learning.'

Quoting researcher Hart he goes on to say, 'Humans never really cognitively understand or learn something ... until they can create a personal metaphor or model.' He adds, 'In a study of readers, Bower and Morrow found that comprehension increased when readers created a mental model or pattern of the material while reading. The readers would make patterns, connections, relating the actions of the characters to their goals.' Some ways of utilizing the pattern-making capacity of the brain are listed below:

To utilize this pattern-making function you should allow students to preview new material by:

- participating in prediction exercises
- making and sharing memory maps of what they already know
- asking them to anticipate links to their own learning goals
- using a creative visualization to realize the topic in their imagination

As part of the progress through new material you can:

- build in individual, pair and group reviews using active listening prompts
- compile a group or class topic web with visual summaries of the content
- summarize via role play, mime or dance

To review for recall and understanding:

- have groups take responsibility for summarizing sections of content
- provide opportunities for students to explain how new content links with learning goals
- let students plan the effective teaching of the topic to others

Dr Roger Sperry's research in the USA on the split brain showed that different sides of the brain controlled different sides of the body and specialized functions. Sperry won a Nobel Prize for his work in 1977. We now know that while both sides of the brain are involved in nearly every human activity, each hemisphere does have some clear-cut specialization.

When the brain is in a relaxed state the electrical activity is in alpha waves of eight to ten cycles per second. Experiments completed by Robert Ornstein showed increases in the levels of electrical cycles in different sides of the brain dependent on the type of mental activity. When subjects were given mathematical problems to solve, the right side relaxed, while activity on the left side increased. Other experiments showed the right hemisphere to be better in the appreciation of depth, recognition of faces and patterning.

Significantly, it began to emerge that the left hemisphere is used in serial processing – identifying units of information in sequence – while the right hemisphere is used more in parallel processing – synthesizing several units of information simultaneously. The advantage to the brain is that each hemisphere can analyse its own type of input first, subsequently exchanging information across the brain via the corpus callosum, once some processing has occurred. Two streams of data are thus integrated to give a balanced and fuller perspective. Tony Buzan claims that when people involve themselves in activities which develop a mental area they previously considered weak, the synergy which results leads to an improvement in all-round mental performance.

Individuals tend to favour one type of processing. You will favour left or right. The students in your class will favour left or right. This has subsequently been confirmed through CAT scan work with patients in hospitals. Scientists can now use radioactive trace elements in the blood to observe and record brain activity during tasks.

It is also worth pointing out that what you teach and how you choose to teach it may also demonstrate your preference for left or right. The summary of the relative lateralization of brain function is given below. As you compare across it may be worth considering what the implications are for learners in your classroom.

Relative lateralization

Left Brain

language
logic
mathematical formulae
number
sequence
linearity
analysis
words of a song
learning from the part to the whole
phonetic reading system
unrelated factual information

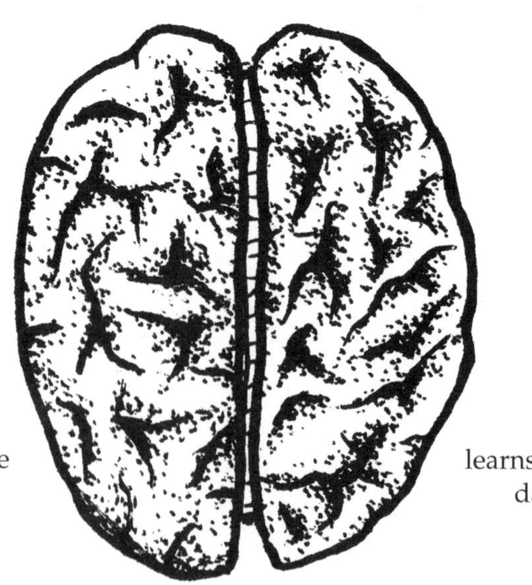

Right Brain

forms and patterns
spatial manipulation
rhythm
musical appreciation
images and pictures
dimension
imagination
tune of song
learns the whole first then parts
daydreaming and visioning
whole language reader
relationships in learning

What are the implications for teaching and learning?

The first and obvious point is that it is no better to be a right-brain or a left-brain learner. Nor is it the case that an individual will align with the processing functions on one side to the complete exclusion of the functions dominated by the other hemisphere. The brain compensates and balances. However, if we all tend towards a preference for one type of processing then it is perhaps the case that we will ourselves make sense of the sensory information in a preferred way and therefore generate our meanings in a preferred way. It also follows that we, as teachers, interpret data, re-present data and provide learning experiences based on that data in our own preferred way.

In a classroom of learners how do we know which are right- and which are left-brain learners? The inevitable answer is that we don't. Is it possible that there will be a mis-match between learner preference and the learning experience being provided? The inevitable answer is yes.

Effective learning based on an understanding of the brain and its design will be whole brain learning. Whole brain learning means recognizing that teaching and learning do not always co-exist and that too much of one sort of diet will impoverish learning. Whole brain learning also means recognizing that the easiest way to reach all of your learners is to provide a balanced diet. Make it varied, nourishing and tasty, plan it beforehand using a recipe book; and talk to the diners afterwards.

The whole brain learning diet should be:

Balanced.

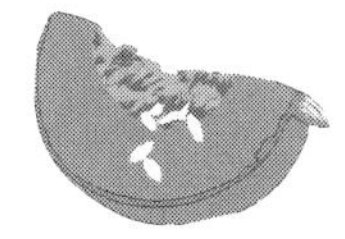

Look at the functions of the left and right brain and consider ways in which you can access learning topics, in ways which will use functions from both sides. Remember that the synergy generated in creating new pathways between left and right results in all-round improvement. When you are applying the multiple intelligences approach described in Section Three, your classroom practice will automatically be left- and right-brain balanced.

Effective, balanced, whole brain learning is rich, multi-path, multi sensory learning. It accesses all the senses and operates at a conscious and unconscious level. You won't overstimulate the brains in your classroom, nor will you exceed their capacity!

Varied.

Break the pattern! Our brain is designed for ups and downs, spurts and plateaux. It is not designed for constant attention. The terms 'on' or 'off' task are unhelpful in whole brain learning. The brain learns best when there are many beginnings and endings, when there are different types of input at different levels and when there are choices. Build in choice or choices wherever possible. Eric Jensen says that the maximum 'on task' time for adults is 20–25 minutes with breaks of 2–5 minutes in between. The best division of time for ten year olds is about 12 minutes of focus time with about 2–5 minutes of individual, paired or group review or play in between.
A six year old is best with about 6 minutes of 'on task' time with about 2–3 away from task.

Nourishing.

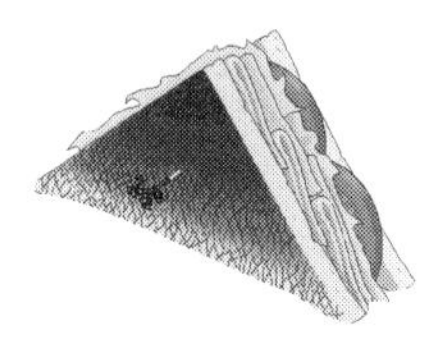

Help the learners see the value in the learning. Use some or all of the goal-setting strategies described in the next section. Be congruent and positive in your expectations of each learner and how you reinforce this verbally and non-verbally. Use every opportunity to give and receive feedback. This can be around rituals in class – break states and affirmations – or in your use of positive strokes or in your management of the reward system.

Tasty.

Make your classroom a learning environment by accessing all the senses – five if possible. Where possible make it colourful, active, musical and bright. Always use visual reinforcement. Place students' work alongside posters with key concepts, flashcards with essential vocabulary and positive affirmation posters. If you are nomadic and don't have your own space adopt the practice by scaling it down. Use flashcards and visuals as an integral art of the lesson. Bring a tape player. Prepare some visuals beforehand; laminate them and use them again.

Recipe Book.

Plan it beforehand. Be aware of your own preferred teaching or presentation styles and those of others around you. Use some of the self audit sheets provided in this book to track the balance of your lessons. Let students know what's coming up. Limit surprises! Try to avoid planning lessons between the door and the desk! Constant and varied pre-exposure will encourage quicker and deeper learning far better than any surprises.

Talk to the diners.

Review it afterwards and during. Involve the students in reviewing the lesson during and after. Use formal and informal approaches. Remember – without feedback you cannot develop or improve your skills. The more varied and useful the feedback the more likely it is that you can continue to improve.

Memory Map of the brain in learning

Review

Key questions about the brain in learning ...

- In what ways can learning relate to the development age of a child?
- What functions do left and right brain control?
- What is the significance of this for learning?
- In what ways might your teaching be left- or right-brained?
- What happens to the brain in stress?
- How does stress affect learning?
- What can you do in your classroom to alleviate learner stress?
- What are the first three things you can do to further develop whole brain learning in your classroom?

Building and maintaining positive self-esteem in the learner

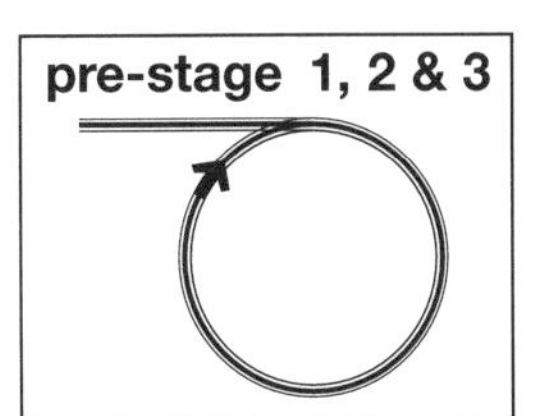

In Section Two you will learn how ...

- ***the BASIS model builds and maintains positive self-esteem and self-belief***
- ***BASIS includes strategies for building the five elements of: Belonging, Aspirations, Safety, Identity and Success***
- ***to set learning goals***
- ***affirming meaningful positive and personal individual goals activates the filtering system within the brain***
- ***positive suggestion improves the chances of learning success***
- ***teacher expectations of the learner are communicated consciously and unconsciously***

Self-esteem and self-belief.

Positive-self esteem and self-belief lie at the core of Accelerated Learning. The learner must believe that there is value in the learning and that he or she is capable of learning and applying it in some meaningful way. Nathaniel Branden, one of the world's leaders in this area says, 'I regard self-esteem as the single most powerful force in our existence ... the way we feel about ourselves affects virtually every aspect of our existence.' He developed a definition of self-esteem as, 'The experience of being competent to cope with the basic challenges of life and being worthy of happiness.'

The development of positive self-esteem and self-belief in learners contributes to the physical condition of relaxed alertness which optimizes learning. It allows learners to set realistic and achievable goals while having a sense of one's own strengths and limitations. Learners with positive self-esteem are less likely to be plagued by self-doubt and the negative self-talk which comes with it. They are less likely to go into stress and exhibit 'reptilian' behaviours. A school, college or training organization which intervenes, at all levels, to build and maintain positive self-esteem and self-belief in learners, takes an important step in increasing the likelihood that new skills and knowledge will be transferable and lifelong.

The Elton Report pointed out the need for schools to make academic work 'winnable' for those whose low self-esteem was threatened by failure:

> *Our evidence suggests that many children who behave badly in school are those whose self-esteem is threatened by failure. They see academic work as 'unwinnable'. They soon realise that the best way to avoid losing in such a competition is not to enter it.*
>
> ***Elton Report 1989***

Many of us carry memories of teachers in our lives who have made a difference; who have made our academic work 'winnable'. For me it includes the primary school teacher who decided that her class wouldn't sit in the order of the last test result. For the first time I got to sit near to the front. It includes the teacher who took an interest in what I did at home and could remember my name from the first day I met her. It includes the secondary teacher who, in his year before retirement, removed me from his class because I talked too much but who nevertheless marked with care all the work that I did on my own as I sat outside in the corridor.

There is a saying that: 'Children don't care how much you know until they know how much you care.' For each of us there will have been teachers who have behaved in all sorts of remarkable and unremarkable ways in classrooms but have touched us, nevertheless, because we sensed that they cared. These convictions stay with us. They are lifelong.

Self-esteem and self-belief are not inherited, they are learned. Children are not born with a positive or negative self-picture, they learn it and that learning is reinforced through the experiences they encounter in their everyday lives. Teachers, like the three I remember with such clarity, make a difference. They can be the still centre in a young person's life. They can impact profoundly on student self-esteem and self-belief. The messages you communicate as one of these teachers will directly influence your students' capacity to learn and achieve.

Self-esteem and self-belief

- ***is learned not inherited***
- ***is reinforced through the everyday experiences of the learner***
- ***is capable of dramatic change***
- ***affects all thinking and all behaviour***
- ***impacts on learning and performance***
- ***can be built and developed with interventions which disrupt the downward cycle of limiting beliefs and negative self-talk***
- ***when low in teachers, will be communicated to learners unconsciously and consciously***

Many Accelerated Learning programmes take the motivation and commitment of the learner for granted. In our model we argue that knowledge of the design of the brain for learning, of how to access the multiple intelligences and create stimulating learning contexts is irrelevant if learners are unable to see, hear or sense themselves being successful in learning. With such a sense of impending achievement, consistently and constantly reinforced, and a connection to some personal and meaningful goal or goals, genuinely accelerative learning can and will take place. To create this level of resourcefulness in the learner it is necessary to provide the following five components. I have described them as the BASIS Model. The model is culled from some of the many and varied programmes which exist in the UK and the United States aimed at building self-esteem in adults and children. All of these programmes have the BASIS elements in common.

The BASIS Model

Belonging

To feel approved of and respected by others, particularly in relationships which are regarded as significant, is what is understood by belonging. Students with a sense of belonging feel as though they belong to a group which is of importance to them. They feel recognized and acknowledged. In such groupings they can experience the importance of trust, loyalty and consistency.

Aspirations

A learner needs to believe that learning has some purpose. A lack of aspiration leads into a downward spiral of negativity. Aspirations provide motivation and a feeling of purpose about life. Learners with aspirations can set realistic and achievable goals and take responsibility for the consequences of decisions relating to their aspirations.

Safety

A feeling of safety or security involves a strong sense of certainty. It can be defined as feeling comfortable and safe within the group, where the expectations and ground rules are known and accepted. Students who feel safe can take risks. Safe environments have clear practices and generally understood roles and responsibilities. Safety also includes the assurance that basic comfort needs will be met.

Identity

A strong sense of identity means that the learner has knowledge of their own strengths and weaknesses, values and beliefs. They have an inner resilience which makes them less susceptible to becoming disillusioned and self-doubting. Identity includes the acquisition of accurate self-knowledge in terms of roles, relationships and attributes, to foster a feeling of individuality. Learners with a strong sense of identity are less likely to experience the counter-productive consequences of negative stress.

Success

Regular and positive affirmation of success – however large or small – reinforces the belief that the learner has control over his or her own life. It helps prevent 'mental drop-out' and it attunes the positive potential of learners. The presence of 'success' in learners is characterized by a feeling of accomplishment in areas regarded as valuable or important. These learners will also have an awareness of their own strengths and be able to place any limitations in context.

Effective schools and teachers reinforce the elements of BASIS at all points. Here is a summary outline of some of the practical ways of doing so both at school and class level.

Belonging

Students with limited skills in this area experience difficulty in making and keeping friends; are often shy; attach their affections inappropriately; seem isolated; and can be insensitive to the emotions and needs of others. Such students are seldom comfortable in groups. Their negative behaviours in class can include bullying; victimizing; showing-off; encouraging cliques; and reticence.

At a school level:

- ➨ encourage a variety of inclusive group activities, some of which are non-competitive
- ➨ instigate a positive behaviour programme and a systematic scheme of rewards
- ➨ monitor instances of bullying and take affirmative action to prevent it
- ➨ use mentoring schemes with senior pupils or outside organizations such as Education Business Partnerships
- ➨ place value on whole group activities such as assemblies

At a classroom level:

- ➨ use a variety of individual, paired and group activities
- ➨ provide opportunities to increase awareness of classmates' families, background and interests
- ➨ foster an identity within your class by emphasizing collective achievements
- ➨ use co-operative learning techniques to build team skills

Aspirations

'The key to self-motivation and purposeful behaviour is to help children internalize goals for themselves and to work towards their attainment.' **(Robert Reasoner)**

Learners who are unable to work towards meaningful goals often lack self-empowerment and appear aimless. Unable to see alternatives or constructive solutions they will often be over-dependent on others, be attention-seeking or manipulative. They may be unwilling or even unable to acknowledge the consequences of their own actions.

At a school level:

- ➨ promote the successes of the school through PR
- ➨ give regular information on progression routes in a planned, systematic way
- ➨ build in goals, interim targets and related tasks to action-planning with students
- ➨ involve parents and/or other adults in goal-setting
- ➨ encourage positive non-judgemental attitudes to counselling among staff

At a classroom level:

- ➨ use decision-making exercises
- ➨ teach problem-solving tools and techniques – for example, flow-charts, force-field analysis
- ➨ refer to and use role-models from the students' own experiences
- ➨ analyse past performance, isolate successes and build on them

Safety

Evidence of learner insecurity can be seen when students avoid lessons, situations within lessons or show disproportionate discomfort with new experiences. Distrust, challenges to authority, insecurity around friendships and over-reliance on particular classmates are also indicative of excessive personal anxiety.

At a school level:

- ensure that all students experience trust-building activities and similar work as part of PSHE
- install a behaviour and reward policy which is consistently applied and on which students have been consulted
- develop staff awareness of positive reinforcement techniques

At a classroom level:

- use trust-building activities
- apply class and school rules fairly and consistently
- see your students and get to know them in different contexts
- avoid put-downs

Identity

'A well defined sense of self and identity provides us with effective strategies for managing psychological stress - the major stress in our society.' **(David Elkind)**

Evidence of weak identity can be seen when the learner is unduly sensitive to criticism, resists participating in any activity in which they risk failure and is unduly anxious to please. Often they will be awkward when praised, either refuting it when offered or becoming embarrassed or being unable to recognize their achievements.

At a school level:

- promote and acclaim individual successes across a wide range of academic and non-academic achievements
- develop regular one-to-one reviews and individual action-planning sessions
- use non-uniform and fancy dress days to allow students and staff to participate together
- monitor the PSHE programme to ensure there are planned opportunities to develop assertiveness and positive self-concepts
- enthuse staff to model the sorts of positive attitudes and behaviours you seek to support

At a classroom level:

- give and seek frequent and fair feedback
- develop a vocabulary and agreed principles for constructive feedback between students
- explore the concepts surrounding identity using collage, time-lines, autobiographies, scrap books, and so on.
- find something unique and positive about every student and let them know it
- provide opportunities – especially for boys – to express emotions

Success

'Students who feel good about themselves and their abilities are the ones who are most likely to succeed.'
(William Purkey)

Students who are convinced they are unlikely to succeed will be unlikely to take risks, contribute ideas or offer opinions. They will frequently lament their own inadequacies and preface statements with 'I'll never' or 'I can't'. They are the students who will often appear frustrated or opt-out of challenging activities.

At a school level:

- send students to the 'office' ... when they are successful!
- discourage student comparisons with other students' work: focus on performance improvement
- break down steps to improvement into small, realizable chunks
- provide formal feedback on performance through a variety of means
- establish 'achievement' days or weeks across the school and promote them through assemblies and form meetings

At a classroom level:

- use strategies such as hobby days or talks for students to display their real interests
- teach active listening skills for giving and receiving feedback
- explain the effects of negative self-talk and how to deal with it
- find an area where your student is guaranteed to succeed and promote it

For these practical approaches to work, the teacher also needs to communicate skilfully and with consistency and self-knowledge.

Positive suggestion and learning success

The accelerated learning classroom is one where success and the possibility of success is affirmed at all levels. Firstly, there is the learning environment itself. This is covered in detail in Section Four and includes classroom layout and organization, use of positive 'affirming' posters and peripherals, management of space, heat and light and the use of music. Secondly, there are the interactions between teacher and learner. These operate at a non-verbal and verbal level as well as a conscious and unconscious level.

Research suggests that in human communication three factors are of most significance: the content of what is said, the tone in which it is said and the non-verbal communication which accompanies it. Some researchers have quantified the relative significance as 9 per cent for the content, 11 per cent for the tone of voice and 80 per cent for the non-verbal accompaniment. It is important for the students in your class that the positive messages you send are congruent. In other words your words of support are matched by supportive body language!

Positive strokes

A stroke is defined as a 'unit of attention'. Humans need them for survival and growth. Without strokes, positive or negative, we wither. Strokes can be given or received, be accepted or discounted, be positive or negative, conditional or unconditional, plastic or real.

A positive stroke is a unit of attention which makes the receiver feel good about him- or herself. A negative stroke has the opposite effect. A survey of 50 Junior Schools in London conducted by Peter Mortimore of the Institute of Education noted that teachers spent less than one per cent of their time giving praise.

Positive	Positive conditional	Negative
'congratulations'	'If you continue to work as hard as this I'll expect you to succeed'	'I'm disappointed in you'
'well done'	'when you complete the homework on time you are one of my best pupils'	'you are letting yourself down'
'that's an excellent piece of work'	'by continuing to ... you will ... and then you ....'	'see me later'
'thank you'	'a big thank you for collecting all those books for me'	'sort yourself out'
'you're working really hard'	'this is the best piece of work so far ... I'm pleased to get it'	'again?'
'this is the best piece of work so far'	'arrived on time again: well done'	'you're not as clever as your mother/father/brother/sister/pet fish'
'you are a credit to the school'	'your mother/father/pet fish would be proud of you'	'you will never ...'
'you are going to succeed'		'you cannot ...'
'I can tell you are confident'		'don't think you ...'
'superb...'		'for once in your life could you ...'

Jack Canfield, a self-esteem consultant and researcher, described the results of a research project where 100 children were observed at school and at home. The children on average received 460 negative or critical comments and 75 positive or supportive comments every day. Aggregated up, imagine the impact it has on their self-belief and their capacity and willingness to achieve!

Strokes can be given unconditionally, 'You have been really enthusiastic in this lesson.' or conditionally , 'I really admire you when you're so enthusiastic in this lesson.' Unconditional strokes have more impact than conditional strokes but are given less frequently.

Strokes can be accepted, 'Thank you, that means a lot to me.' or discounted, 'Thank you, but it's no more than anyone else really.' Many individuals spend their lives discounting strokes and have developed sophisticated ways of doing so.

Strokes can be real, 'I do enjoy having you in my lessons.' or plastic. A plastic stroke can look and sound real but somehow doesn't feel real 'I do enjoy having you in my lessons!' Often this depends on the congruence exhibited.

The teacher can create a regime where there are no negative strokes and no put downs. Teachers, aware of the differing impact of 'strokes' can make interventions to encourage more unconditional positive strokes which are accepted and not discounted. In the 'no-put down zone' positive reinforcement displaces name-calling and negative talk. Students are encouraged to develop skills to counter the put-downs.

Research using the Transactional Analysis techniques has shown that to influence changes in behaviour a regime of four positive strokes in favour of one negative has a powerful impact. In the Accelerated Learning classroom there are at least four positive strokes to each negative one as well as a balance in favour of unconditional over conditional. Where a teacher's message is congruent no strokes are plastic!

By using 'affirming' messages on displays around the classroom and school, posters of role models and developing a positive reinforcement vocabulary, learners can be helped to 'believe they can achieve'. Affirming messages for your class could include some of the following examples.

I am successful in overcoming obstacles

I will succeed today

I am receptive and ready to learn

Learning is enjoyable and worthwhile

Our greatest advantage is our ability to learn

Affirmations are positive, personal and unconditional statements which reinforce goal-setting and a sense of achievement. Repeating affirmations engages the 'self-convincing' process within the limbic system which Dr Paul McLean identified in his triune brain research. Neuro-Linguistic Programming (NLP) research has modelled criteria for the brain to be self-convinced. Affirmations must be reinforced in the dependent modality – visual, auditory or kinesthetic. Affirmations require frequent and further reinforcement over time. Positive and personal affirmations are a key outcome of the process of setting learning goals.

Strategies for setting personal learning goals

In an article headlined: *'Sink Schools Taught To Excel'* (*Observer*, 11 February 1996) - the headteacher of a school in the north-west of England which is described as, 'Taking underachievers at the age of 11 and turning them into overachievers', says
'It is a mission with me that any student can succeed. Day in day out we tell our students that they are going to succeed. There is no such thing as can't. The school is organised for them to succeed.'

Later the same article describes the significance of goal-setting: 'Setting goals is also vital – students are given weekly homework goals, teachers are set goals, entire forms are given exam goals.'

A goal is 'a dream with a timescale'. It is aspirational. It engages the limbic system within the brain. When a powerful personal goal is set and affirmed, the brain begins to operate in ways which helps that goal be delivered. The reticular formation filters useful information in and useless information out. For example, if you decide that your goal is to obtain a new job or buy a new car or to learn a foreign language you will, when you commit to that goal, begin to behave in ways to help you meet that goal. This happens consciously but also unconsciously. When you make a positive personal commitment to find a new job you will find yourself hearing conversations about career moves, see recruitment ads and catch yourself 'feeling' what it might be like in your desired job.

If you decide to replace your old car with a newer model and have in mind a specific type and specific colour, you begin to notice them from the minute you drive out of the staff car park! If you are thinking of learning a foreign language, before you know it you will be catching news items about that country and seeing advertisements for evening classes and correspondence courses!

To engage powerful and personal goals with the learners in your class, the goals must be theirs, not yours or the school's. Goals are different from targets or tasks. A goal is powerful and compelling. Once it is set it is attractive. Targets are the significant landmarks on the journey towards the goal. Tasks are what you do to meet your targets. This distinction is an important one for teachers working with learners who are sometimes unable to see what's in it for them. For example:

Goal	Targets	Tasks
'I will be happy in a well-paid job in two years' time.'	• obtain credit at GNVQ by June of next year	• complete current coursework on time • get two good work experience placements • draw up a homework and revision schedule
	• have a quality portfolio with a detailed CV and examples of my artwork to take to interviews by December	• plan contents and clear out poor work • look at other examples • speak to teachers and lecturers
	• by September I'll have a final list of five places I'll visit personally to ask about placements	• list all the possibilities and put them in priority • write to the top ten • phone them
	• agree a monthly series of meetings with my tutor to check work is complete/good enough	• change my shift at the superstore for meetings • make sure driving lessons don't clash

Goal	Targets	Tasks
'By the end of this year I will be so confident and knowledgeable that I can choose the best college course for me.'	• to give a ten minute assembly without notes by December	• practise on my own at home • do a memory map of the topic • visit the zoo and meet the researcher
	• have visited all the local colleges and met the Head of Department by September	• collect the course booklets • buy a diary • phone them up and do it!!
	• gone on a trekking holiday with Ali and Jez in half-term and paid for it myself	• visit travel agents on Saturday • check bank balance and open special account • get fit first
	• have a study plan successfully running from now to exam time	• get to all the study skills lessons (on time) • buy that book on memory techniques - read it • clear out the spare room and put a heater in • make sure that all the notes are filed, reviewed and put the memory maps onto A3
	• get at least three Cs in mock exams	• set aside Mondays – Thursdays 6.00-9.00 • take the books when I'm babysitting • stick the revision timetable in the kitchen • ask about extra help in physics

Goal setting and VAK

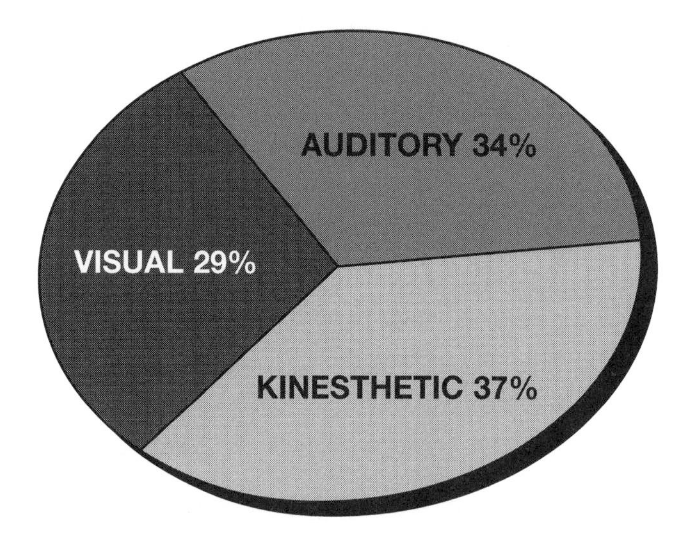

Learner goals are most effective when first described in the dominant modality or modalities. By this we mean either visually, auditorily or kinesthetically or in combinations of these. We all experience the world around us through our senses. Modelling research done in Neuro-Lingustic Programming (NLP) suggests that we each have different preferred 'systems' or 'modalities'. Through our preferred system we interpret and re-interpret our everyday experiences.

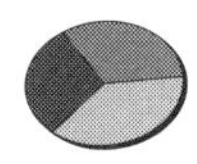

The 29 per cent of us who have a visual preference will be able to 'see' our desired goal and re-create it in pictures, still and moving visual images and imagined scenes. For others this may be difficult. When, as a teacher, you say to your class, 'Now imagine this...' or, 'Can you see what I mean?' or, 'Picture this in your minds eye...' this will be very easy for some, difficult for others, almost impossible for a few.

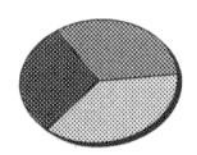

The 34 per cent of us who have an auditory preference will be most receptive to what others are saying on the achievement of our desired goal. Internal dialogue is very easy for this group. What is said, who is saying it and how it is being said will enliven their learning. The teacher who uses phrases like, 'How does this sound to you?' or, 'Ask yourselves this' or, 'Do you hear what I'm saying?' will be communicating directly with this group.

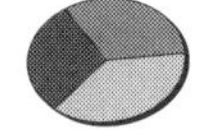

Thirty seven per cent have a kinesthetic preference. This group will best access their learning goals by experiencing the 'feelings' associated with success. They may be the group who will be able to utilize time-line strategies to help them experience success in achieving their goal. A teacher who is herself kinesthetic will use phrases like, 'How does this feel to you?' or, 'I can't get to grips with this' or, 'I'm touched by what you say.'

To help learners set positive personal goals, the first step is to get them to describe their goal in their preferred system. If you don't know their preferred system ask them to answer the question, 'What will the successful achievement of your goal look, sound and feel like?'

A simple checklist of questions which can be used by classroom teachers, pastoral tutors, careers teachers, guidance counsellors or pupils themselves is summarized in the PACES model which is used in NLP to establish 'well-formed outcomes'.

P	**Positive**	What do you want? (stated in the positive)
A	**Achievement**	How would you know you had successfully achieved it? What would you see, hear and feel? How would someone else know you had achieved it?
C	**Context**	When do you want it by? Where? With whom?
E	**Effects**	What would happen if you got it? If you got it would you lose anything? If you could have it now would you take it?
S	**Sustained**	If you get it can you keep it? What would help you keep it?

To help in this process you should provide a selection of keywords which can be used to help select answers. These keywords can be written out onto card and placed on the walls around the room. They can also be put onto A5 and laminated for use in lessons. Some examples are:

positive, confident, certain, relaxed, secure, calm, satisfied, successful, valued, mature, fulfilled, determined, self-reliant, independent, caring, happy, respected, trusted, individual, loved, worthy, approved, partnership, loyal.

Some of the following approaches can be used to help individuals, pairs or groups to set learning goals. They are useful for experiencing the goal in ways other than through the written word.

Visual

Questions to ask
'What will you be seeing when you achieve your goal?'
'Can you describe what the succeesful achievement of our goal looks like?'
'When you imagine success what sorts of things do you see?'
'Picture yourself being successful. What do you see?'

Poster or collage
A visual representation of 'success' either drawn or cut and pasted together encourages thinking about the elements of success.

Visualization
Learners can be encouraged to visualize their goals either as static or moving images: learners can play with the size, colour, depth and brightness of the images.

Appearing in your own movie
By seeing themselves 'captured' on screen (via their mind's eye) learners can manipulate their character and make choices about outcomes.
Simply describing the 'action' can lead to further clarity.

Auditory

Questions to ask

'What will others be saying to you when you are successful?'
'What words come to mind when you think about success?'
'What do you hear when you think of yourself successfully achieving your goal?'

Key phrases

List the words or phrases which epitomise success.

Giving advice from the future

Step forward into the future and from a position of success give your present self advice about how to achieve it

Kinesthetic

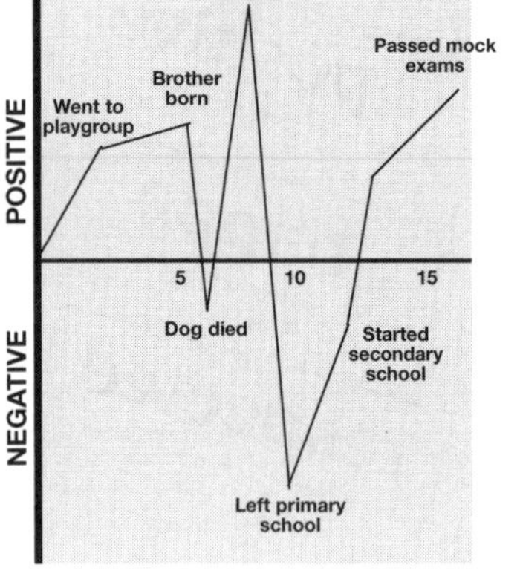

Questions to ask

'What sorts of things will you be doing when you are successful?'
'What sorts of things will you be doing when you've achieved your goal that you are not doing now?'
'What does success feel like? What emotions do you experience?'

Autobiographical time-line

By using a large sheet of paper on which a single horizontal line across the centre represents the learner's lifespan and a vertical axis above and below the line represents positive or negative experiences. Specific past or possible future experiences can be plotted in turn. This helps learners reflect and speculate.

Future-basing

Physically walk on a line which represents the period of time until the successful achievement of the goal. From this position in the future, experience success. What does it look, sound and feel like? Look back down the line and think back to what you had to do to achieve your 'present' successful position. Describe each step in words while staying in the 'future' base.

Sequencing activity

Describe each target or task towards the successful achievement of the goal in words or pictures on index cards. Arrange the cards in sequence. Explain the sequence to someone else.

Setting individual learner goals via targets and tasks

The goal-setting activities help participants be more aware of what success will be like. They also help to make the steps required more explicit. Goals are delivered by achieving specified targets which detail the successive steps one reaches in working towards the goal. Each target will have a set of related tasks. Both targets and tasks can be specified using SMART +.

S	pecific
M	easurable
A	greed
R	eal
T	ime-based
+	plus means stated positively

EXAMPLE *'I don't want to be stuck doing a course I don't like.'*

Sample dialogue

Positive

Q. 'What do you want?'
A. 'I don't want to be stuck doing a course I don't like.'
Q. 'What would you prefer?'
A. 'I'd prefer to be doing a good course that I'd enjoy.'
Q. 'And if you were doing a good course that you enjoyed, what would that do for you?'
A. 'I'd be feeling that it was useful ... that I was going somewhere.'

Achievement

Q. 'How would you know you had successfully got onto a good course?'
A. 'Dunno. Not sure really.'
Q. 'Well, imagine you are on a good course and you are enjoying it. What do you see yourself doing?'
A. 'I'd be laughing ... made some friends ... doing the work ... not worried.'
Q. 'What sorts of things are being said to you?'
A. 'I suppose people are saying that I look content. Yes, I can hear myself speaking up in the class.'
Q. 'So when you are successful and confident in a good course, what are you feeling?'
A. 'I'm looking forward to going in. I'm not depressed any more. It's OK.'
Q. 'How would someone else know you were successful and confident?'
A. 'Maybe I'd be more cheerful and have got some good friends. They'd see me around more.'

Context

Q. 'So you want to be on a good course, enjoying it, have some good friends and be doing the work?'
A. 'Yes, definitely.'
Q. 'Anything else?'
A. 'Confident, not embarrassed so much.'
Q. 'OK. When do you want to be confident and enjoying a good course with new friends by?'
A. 'I want to be in the course for next September.'
Q. 'And the rest?'
A. 'It would be good if I was a bit more confident already!'
Q. 'What would being confident do for you?'
A. 'I wouldn't get embarrassed and tongue-tied. I'd go out more.'
Q. 'And if you weren't so embarrassed and tongue-tied what would that do for you?'
A. 'I'd be able to speak up for myself. I'd make my own decisions then.'
Q. 'So what you want is to be confident enough to make your own decisions?'
A. 'Yes.'
Q. 'And if you could make your own decisions what would that do for you?'
A. 'Well what I really want to do is engineering at Churchfield College.'
Q. 'What is preventing you from doing engineering at Churchfield?'
A. 'Dunno really. I don't think I'll get the grades. No one else thinks it's any good. I'm not sure.'

Effects Q. 'What would happen if you made your own decision about the course?'
A. 'I suppose I'd have to look into it a lot more carefully. Just in case.
But at least it'd be mine then.'
Q. 'If you could begin to make the decision now would you do it?'
A. 'I suppose so...'
Q. 'Suppose?'
A. 'Well yes, if I could begin to make the decision now I'd go ahead.'
Q. 'What's stopping you?'
A. 'Nothing really. I need all the information. I need to research it. I need the grades.'

Sustained Q. 'What would help you get all of this and be confident about it?'
A. 'I need to start. Do a bit at a time. Maybe have a plan. Visit the college....'

'By the end of this year I will be so confident and knowledgeable that I can choose the best college course for me.'

With the goal clearer in the student's mind, the final answer 'I need to start. Do a bit at a time. Maybe have a plan. Visit the college.' can all be given targets which are SMART+.

"By September I will have visited all the Colleges within 45 mins travelling time, met the Head of Engineering, discussed their courses and shown them my portfolio.'

S	pecific	'discussed their courses and shown them my portfolio'
M	easurable	'all the Colleges within 45 mins travelling time'
A	greed..........................	'met the Head of Engineering'
R	eal	'I will have'
T	ime-based	'by September'
+	stated positively.	

Anchoring positive resource states

Anchoring is a term derived from NLP to describe a process where an individual can access a desired state of mind – confidence, calm, excitement, strength – at will. Just as the recollection of negative experiences provokes related negative symptoms – stress, fast heart beat, perspiration, feelings of discomfort – so can the opposite and positive impact be accessed.

Anchoring works by utilizing a stimulus to evoke a consistent response pattern. The stimulus received can be in any one of the five senses individually or in combination. Any one element of an experience tends to bring back the entire experience. You may experience the negative side of this if you have a phobia. The word aeroplane might immediately evoke images of crashes and a related sense of helplessness. For some it's spiders, for others public speaking. For many adults it's school and schools! The negative associations some adults have, return as soon as they walk into the hall on a parents' evening. Marcel Proust described the process in loving detail in *à la recherche du temps perdu*. For him the taste and smell of madeleine cakes brings back all the sensory associations with a moment in his childhood.

Anchoring can be used to access any positive state of mind we need at any given time. We utilise new knowledge about the processing patterns of the brain to help make positive associations. We can reproduce internal states and external behaviours in ourselves by anchoring. Learners can be helped to feel positive about themselves and about potentially stressful experiences such as interviews and exams by using the anchoring technique.

For anchoring to occur, certain conditions must be present:

☞ the person must be relaxed and able to recall an experience which corresponds to the state of mind they seek, for example, a time in their past when they were feeling supremely confident
☞ to help someone to anchor, mirror their body language, breathe at their rate, modulate your voice to match theirs, give your instructions when they are ready for them
☞ the anchor – a touch, vocal characteristic, gesture or movement – must be unique
☞ the anchor must be timed to coincide with full association with the original experience
☞ the anchor can be created in any representational system (VAK)

To help a learner anchor a positive state of mind, first get them to relax. Remove distractions. Encourage the learner to fully relax his or her body before re-creating for themselves a time when they experienced the desired state. This may be a time when they were happy or confident or successful or enthused. Encourage them to access a specific memory when such a 'feeling' was present. While maintaining rapport with them, ask them to re-create the sights, sounds and feelings of that specific time. What could they see? What were they doing? What was being said? How did they feel? What was the physical reaction at the time? At some point their physiology will change as they remember the experience in full. Providing they are fully associated – that is, in the experience themselves and not watching themselves as in a movie – there will be a point when the associated physiology returns and at this point the anchor – a touch or gesture such as squeezing a wrist or finger – should be self-applied. At the same time a movement or sound can be made to reinforce the moment. Do this three or four times. Have your learner practise at home or elsewhere. Do it regularly. There will very quickly come a point when 'firing' the anchor will bring all the positive associations, including the desired state of mind, automatically.

Examination rooms often carry negative associations for students. Before a series of exams is about to take place you can help change these negative associations by taking the students to the examination room and using the anchoring techniques to create positive associations of success and confidence. This will help ease stress and anxiety which could otherwise inhibit performance

Memory Map of building and maintaining postive self-esteem

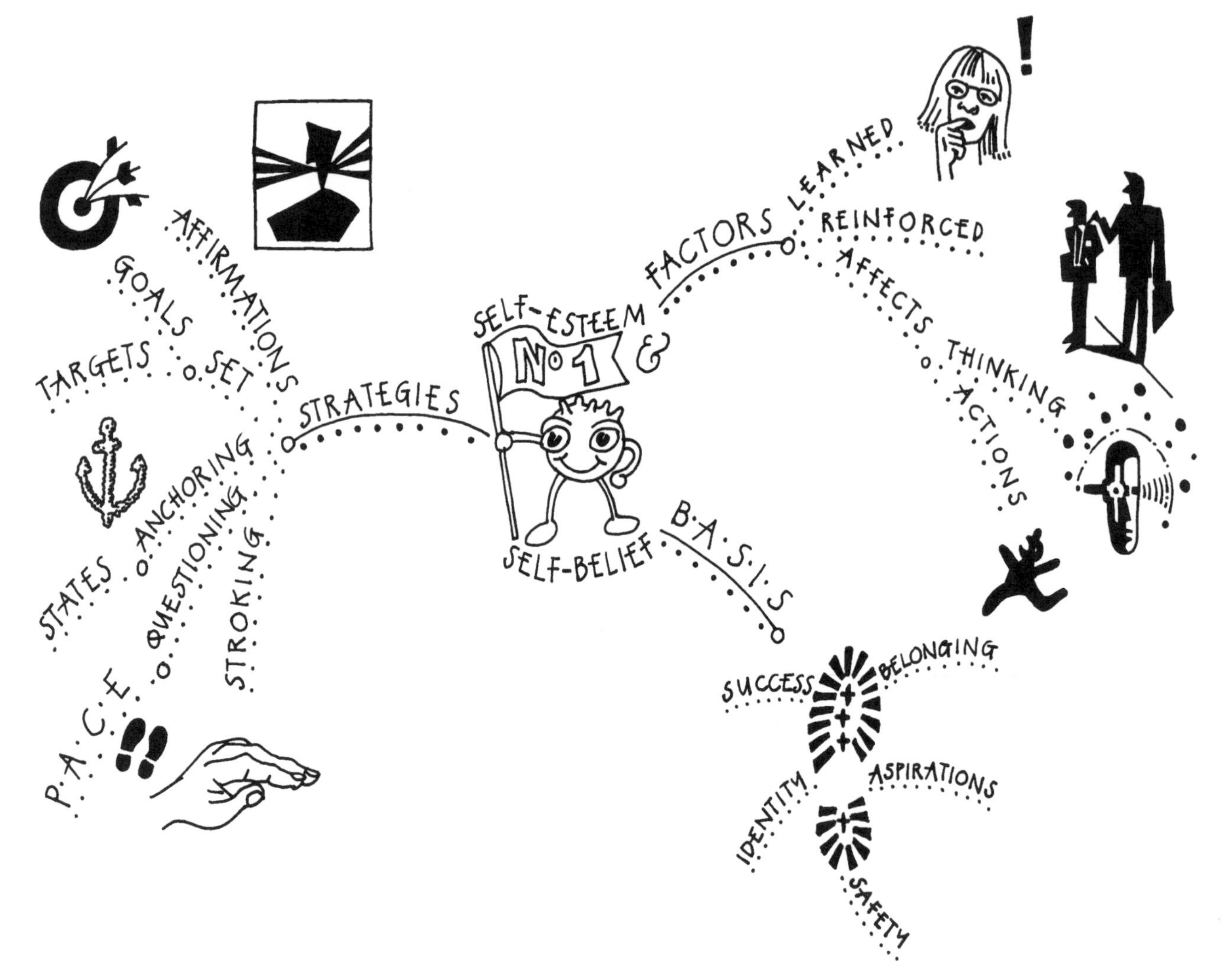

Review

Key questions about building and maintaining self-esteem

- in what ways can positive self-esteem and self-belief be said to be at the core of accelerated learning?
- what practical actions at a school level are possible to introduce BASIS?
- what are the first steps you need to take to introduce some more of the BASIS principles into your classroom practice?
- how can positive suggestion support learner success?
- in what ways can your use of positive strokes be improved?
- what actions need to take place for individual learner goals to be agreed and supported?

Models of learning

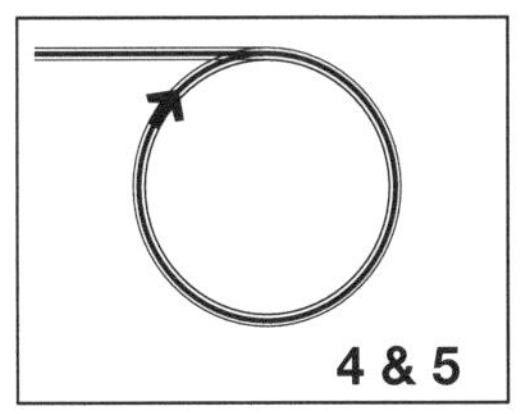

In Section Three you will learn how ...

- ***we each learn through a different balance of visual, auditory and kinesthetic stimulation***
- ***recent theories of learning show important similarities***
- ***Howard Gardner's theory of multiple intelligences underpins Accelerated Learning***
- ***to apply methods of multiple intelligence theory in your classroom***
- ***the Accelerated Learning Cycle includes seven stages and builds on researched understanding about learning***
- ***teaching can and ought to utilize V, A and K stimulus, range across the seven intelligences and work through the stages of the Accelerated Learning Cycle***

'What we are about is learning not teaching, why aren't the research findings about how we learn being put into practice?'

Sir Geoffery Holland, CRAC Conference, January 1996

Learning through the senses: representational systems

Many years of Neuro-Linguistic Programming work in modelling communication strategies has shown that, just as we receive information about the world around us through our five senses, we also have individual sensory preference as to how we re-create and make sense of that information. For some individuals it will be a visual preference, for others auditory and for others kinesthetic. Although when we process information internally we can use any of the five senses to do so, visual, auditory and kinesthetic systems predominate. This is what we mean by VAK.

Have you ever been in a situation where, with a partner, family member or friend, you go to look at a new house? As you walk around the empty rooms you hear the words, 'I can just see our furniture fitting perfectly in this room... we can have the three piece suite over here and...' But try as you might you are unable to visualize the arrangement? Perhaps you need to work it out on paper with dimensions and shapes to scale? Perhaps you physically need to experiment with moving the furniture around? Perhaps you need to have it explained to you in more detail? For some a visualized scene comes easily. For others it is more difficult.

A preferred sensory system does not mean that the individual cannot access or use other systems. Nor is one type of system better. There will, however, be a tendency to favour a certain system. The preference will be out of consciousness. You will not know why you are able to envisage scenes in colourful pictures or hear very distinct associated sounds or have powerful emotions attached to an idea or place. Given that there are such preferences it is possible that others can be developed. It is possible to help learners develop the skills of visualization or an inner-voice or emotional associations, but the preference is likely to remain.

A person with a **visual preference** will readily construct imagined scenes. They will readily 'see' themselves operating in different contexts. They will often see images associated with words or feelings and they will affirm their understanding of new information only when they see it happen or see it written or described visually. When spelling they may 'see' the word as they are about to write it out. An **auditory preference** will be 'expressed' through a preference for internal dialogue and through language generally. Such a person may 'hear' the word spelled out before writing it. In anticipating themselves in a new situation there may be mental rehearsal of what will be said by and to them. A **kinesthetic preference** will come with strong attachment to 'feelings' – emotions or tactile sensations. In spelling a word such a person may 'feel' themselves writing it letter by letter beforehand or it may simply feel right. An anticipated experience will come with strong emotional associations. They will experience the physical situation with all the related emotions that brings.

The preferred representation system can be discerned through noticing different cues. Some of the cues are physiological while others relate to language. The rough summary below begins to give you a picture/feel for/sounding of the fascination of this area. Against the representation system it lists the accompanying physical signs and the sort of linguistic predicates which are likely to be used by the learner and which a teacher, in turn, can use to communicate in the same representational system.

Representational system	Physiology	Language
Visual	• eye movements upwards • breathing high in the chest • high pitched tonality • shallow breathing • accesses information by looking up	*'I see what you mean'* *'That looks good'* *'Can you imagine this?'* *'Picture yourself...'* *'How does this look?'*
Auditory	• eye movements level • even breathing in diaphragm • clear, resonant tonality • even muscle tension • accesses information with head tilted	*'I hear you'* *'Sounds good to me'* *'That rings a bell'* *'Something tells me'* *'How does this sound?'*
Kinesthetic	• eye movement downwards • deep, low breathing in stomach area • voice is more breathy • lots of movement • accesses information while looking down	*'It doesn't feel right'* *'Can you grasp this?'* *'I'm not in touch with...'* *'Change your standpoint'* *'I'm up against it'*

A further way of accessing the preferred systems of the learners in your class is to use a simple test. The example shown on page 44 is from Lawrence Weston School in Bristol where the headteacher, Chris Lindop, has used it with all his pupils. By reading out five sets of ten words in an even and regular tempo and having the learners ring their response they and you are given a quick summary of their VAK preference. Explain beforehand that they must ring the response which corresponds to the first thing that comes into their head. Do they see a picture associated with the word? Do they see a picture of the word? Do they hear the sound of the word repeated with no picture? Does the word evoke a feeling? A sample ten words could include: glass, house, mother, newspaper, love, boat, sun, examination, choice, car. After each ten words have a little mini break-state to get them out of a pattern of responses. Ask them, for example, to turn to their neighbour and say what they did last night. Give them thirty seconds then restart. Add another four sets of ten of your own to my list noticing the different types of words and try it out.

Another good way of accessing a learner's preferred style, while also encouraging some further thinking on their part, is given in the example on page 45 from Pen Park School, Bristol. There, the teachers, Chris Wardle and Jose Verity, use a Learning Choices Questionnaire to encourage discussion and discovery about the different ways of learning.

As a teacher you need to access all the learners in your class. This can be done by utilizing VAK in all your inputs. Be aware that you will have a preferred system and that you will tend to teach through it. If you know this you can do something about it. If you don't then you will remain in your comfort zone.

In your choice of language be sensitive to the predicates you use. Do you rely on, 'I want you to imagine?' or, 'Picture the scene'...? Can you think of ways in which you can make your language multi-sensory? For a visual learner the phrase, 'You won't find the answer on the ceiling.' may be a profound misunderstanding! That may be exactly where, in their visual field, the answer is!

In your choice of inputs be aware of your preferred means. Some examples of VAK approaches are outlined below.

Visual

- **The use of yourself and your body movements,**
- **Utilizing the visual display opportunities above eye level within the room**
- **Video, OHP, slides, flip chart, coloured board markers or chalks**
- **Lively and engaging textbooks**
- **Memory mapping, collage and visual note-taking tools**
- **Keywords displayed around the room**

Auditory

- **Paired and group discussions, group reviews**
- **Guest speakers**
- **Mini-debates**
- **Raps, rhyme, chants and verse, dramatic readings**
- **Tape, sound-bites**
- **Mnemonics, onomatopoeia**
- **Music for energizing, relaxing, visualizing and review**

50 Word Activity

Ring the reaction you have

Word Number	Picture	Picture of word	Sound	Feeling
1	A	B	C	D
2	A	B	C	D
3	A	B	C	D
4	A	B	C	D
5	A	B	C	D
6	A	B	C	D
7	A	B	C	D
8	A	B	C	D
9	A	B	C	D
10	A	B	C	D
11	A	B	C	D
12	A	B	C	D
13	A	B	C	D
14	A	B	C	D
15	A	B	C	D
16	A	B	C	D
17	A	B	C	D
18	A	B	C	D
19	A	B	C	D
20	A	B	C	D
21	A	B	C	D
22	A	B	C	D
23	A	B	C	D
24	A	B	C	D
25	A	B	C	D
26	A	B	C	D
27	A	B	C	D
28	A	B	C	D
29	A	B	C	D
30	A	B	C	D
31	A	B	C	D
32	A	B	C	D
33	A	B	C	D
34	A	B	C	D
35	A	B	C	D
36	A	B	C	D
37	A	B	C	D
38	A	B	C	D
39	A	B	C	D
40	A	B	C	D
41	A	B	C	D
42	A	B	C	D
43	A	B	C	D
44	A	B	C	D
45	A	B	C	D
46	A	B	C	D
47	A	B	C	D
48	A	B	C	D
49	A	B	C	D
50	A	B	C	D
Total				

Add up how many times you ringed each letter and enter the total.

Learning Style Preference

Working out your learning style preferences.

		A high number of responses of this type. *Means this is your learning preference.*	*A high number would be:*	*An average number would be:*
A	☐	**Visual**	**30+**	**12–18**
B	☐	**Verbal/** ***visual*** ***(seeing words)***	**16+**	**9–12**
C	☐	**Auditory** ***(hearing)***	**16+**	**9–12**
D	☐	**Physical** ***(feeling)***	**18+**	**8–12**

Name

Look at the **THING TO LEARN** then decide if you would prefer **CHOICE A, CHOICE B or CHOICE C** as a way to learn it. Put a tick in the box to make your choice.

THINGS TO LEARN	CHOICE A		CHOICE B		CHOICE C	
Times table	Cover over and picture it		Saying out aloud		Adding on fingers	
Spelling a word	Write it down		Imagine what it looks like		Say each letter out	
Learning a foreign word	Repeating it out loud to yourself		Writing it out over and over again		Looking at a picture next to the word	
Learning a history fact	Watch a video		Listen to a person on the radio explaining what happened		Role play - act out what happened	
Learning how something works	Take the object apart and try to put it back together		Look at a diagram or a picture on the board		Listen to a speaker telling you about it	
Learning a story	Tell someone else the story		Draw pictures/cartoons to tell the story		Imagine the story	
Learning a new sport	Watch a demonstration		Repeat back instructions to the coach		Do it	
Learning a new move on a trampoline	Let the coach support you through the movements so you feel how to do it		Look at diagrams of the move on cards (flashcards)		Talk through the movements with a friend	
Learning how to use a new tool in the workshop	Listen to your friend explain how to use it		Teach someone else how to use it		Watch someone else use it	
Learning how to make a cake	Look at the instructions on the packet		Listen to a tape about what to do		Try to make it	
Learning to count in a foreign language	Sing the words		Look at cards/posters		Play French bingo	
Learning how the eye works	Listen to a doctor telling you		Make a model		Look at a diagram of the eye	

Kinesthetic

- **Body sculpture, mime**
- **Gestures or movements learned to demonstrate a concept**
- **Break-state activities**
- **Design and build activities**
- **Field trips and visits**
- **Physical movement for example, Brownian motion illustrated by students bumping together in a confined space; maps drawn on hard play areas to help learn countries and trade routes**

In the Accelerated Learning Cycle input via VAK is important. If you are self-consciously auditing your teaching to ensure that there is a balance then you are begining to access your students in their preferred learning style.

Four learners

When we consider the learners whom, as teachers, trainers and lecturers, we encounter on a daily basis, we can begin to appreciate that their learning needs are different. If you think of those whom you teach you may have a strong sense of their different personalities, their patterns of behaviour, character quirks and idiosyncrasies. You will have a sense of their potential based on personal and professional judgements. You may even have an appreciation of which learning experiences they prefer. Yet it could be that you did not have any real idea of how those same learners learn most effectively. As you read and consider the profiles of the different learners outlined below, ask yourself if there are others like them in your classes and if there are, how do you know? How do you provide learning which meets their individual needs?

Lindsey

prefers:

Working on own at home. Will spend a lot of time on self-directed tasks. Working early in the day and for an extended time on task. Irregular breaks. To contribute to team activities as an 'expert' or 'completer-finisher'.

enjoys:

Left brain activities puzzles, logic problems, sequencing tasks. Discipline of routine and planning in advance. Detailed, completed work. Single outcomes and solutions. Responsibility of completing task independently. Adult company. Abstractions and conceptualization.

wants:

Quiet. Deadlines. Own space/desk, chair, filing system. Own time for reflection.

Lara

prefers:

To work with a partner or with close supervision or to regularly reviewed deadlines. Small units of work and immediate feedback. Hard chair and large table space.

enjoys:

Right brain activities, reassurance of the Big Picture, clear connections to previous learning. Likes to use lots of tools to break work down – for example, post-its, index cards, flow charts. Visual learning.

wants:

Discipline of timetable with reward system. Space away from domestic regime – for example, library, school study room.

Lennie

prefers:
Kinesthetic and hands on learning. Repetition of the experience. Evidence of the value of the learning.

enjoys:
Simulations and role play. Trial and error. Practical activity. Shared responsibility.

wants:
Support to alleviate high anxiety about learning. Keywords. Visual spelling reinforcement

Li

prefers:
Cramming before exams and given deadlines. Likes to work late and with gentle background music. Open-ended problems. Hypothesizing.

enjoys:
Taping key learning on personal stereo. Using rote learning and revising key concepts auditorily. Class discussion Group tasks, research involving communication skills.

wants:
Pressure of deadlines. External motivation. Whole brain access to content.

The Accelerated Learning approach is a systematic way of ensuring that such different learning needs can be met. It is tested against well researched models of learning.

Models of learning

'Every human being has a learning style and every human being has strengths.'
Professors Ken and Rita Dunn

The Accelerated Learning approach is underpinned by models of learning which show similarities and which have been thoroughly researched over time. These models of 'learning styles' help remind us that each learner is unique in the way he or she makes sense of the world and approaches educational experiences. No one way of 'learning' will always be better at all times nor can learners choose their preferred learning style. An individual's learning will be the outcome of the evolving dynamic between the brain (the hard-wiring) and how it makes sense of the experiences provided for it (the signals).

Learning style is identified by Dunn and Dunn as being: 'That consistent pattern of behaviour and performance by which an individual approaches educational experiences.' As such it is best looked at as a composite of influencing factors, some of which a teacher can control and others which are beyond the teacher's control. A learner will have a characteristic way of perceiving, interacting and responding to the learning environment and this will have been shaped by cognitive and affective factors, the deep structure of neural organization and those 'environmental' experiences such as home, school and culture. Models of learning offer a mechanism for comparing such a composite of characteristics against others. They provide a neat categorization which continues to remind us that each learner may learn differently and not necessarily in the ways in which we, as teachers, would expect or, more significantly, can access readily through our teaching. The models are not in themselves 'true'. They are a means of ordering and categorizing. Models of learning styles are simply mechanisms of categorizing and making sense of some of the ways we currently observe students' learning.

Understanding different models of learning can help students better appreciate some of their own preferences. Teachers should use early opportunities to assist in understanding what factors contribute to different preferences and what those preferences might be. In doing this, teachers will become more attuned to the needs of their students and to their own teaching strategies for meeting these needs. An additional and more useful product of assessing learning styles is in helping students develop techniques to adopt and adapt their own ways of learning. When teachers do this they are providing lifelong learning.

Dunn and Dunn's Learning Styles Model isolates factors which contribute to a person's preferred learning style. It is no coincidence that the factors or elements they isolate are all key concerns in designing the Accelerated Learning experience.

Dunn and Dunn's model identifies five categories in which they place elements which all contribute to an individual's preferred learning profile. The categories are: environmental, emotional, sociological, physical and psychological. Within each category the 'elements' impact on the overall learner profile. So, for example, their environmental category includes the elements of sound, light, temperature and room design or layout. Preferences within each of these elements will distinguish the learner. Do you prefer quiet, background noise or loud music in your ideal learning environment? Do you learn best in artificial or natural light? In the cold or in the warmth? Do you prefer learning at a table or desk or in a soft chair?

Dunn and Dunn's Learning Styles Model

Ken and Rita Dunn's Learning Styles Inventory can be used with your classes. Use their categories and elements to stimulate your students' thinking about their own preferred patterns of learning. Applications could include structured pair and group discussions around the elements, a research project outlining the class or individual profiles. Or graphically the construction of a collage, photo-album, autobiography, song or rap which 'celebrates' the individualism of each learner, group of learners or class. Another activity to encourage thinking about learning is to use a guided visualization using each element as a point on the journey. Used with the text as described below, this could help begin to provide students with answers prior to some of the reporting activities.

Finding out how you best enjoy learning: a guided visualization

'As you listen to the music, I'd like you to relax. Feel the soles of your feet on the floor, settle down and prepare to enjoy a journey. You may close your eyes if you wish. Breathe deeply. As you listen to the music, relax from the top of your head to the soles of your feet. Enjoy the feeling. ...Pause... We are about to begin a journey to explore how you enjoy learning best. When we return you'll know all you need to know to help you begin to learn successfully. ...Pause... As you relax your eyes and your mouth and your ears and your neck continue to breathe deeply and enjoy the music.

Take yourself to a place where you enjoy learning. Enjoy the sights and sounds of being there. As you continue to relax and listen to the music, enjoy the sounds as you learn successfully. Whether your place is light or dark or warm or cool, you can feel success as a learner when you are there. When you are being even more successful as a learner enjoy the experience, continue to relax, asking yourself what is it that is making me so successful here? Is the learning fun? What is making it fun? Is it useful? In what ways is it useful? ...Pause...As you continue to relax and see and hear and feel yourself being a successful learner, how are others helping you be successful? Breathe deeply, listen to the music ... And as you enjoy being in your perfect learning place, ask yourself what's the best time of day for me to be learning?

As you enjoy the music and continue to breathe deeply you may like to think a little more about how you learn best... what sort of things do you enjoy doing as you learn? Think of the subject which you learn best. What is it you do in that subject that helps you more than anything else? And as you continue to breathe deeply, enjoying the music and your successes in learning spend some time there ...Pause... before preparing to come back with all the secrets of your learning successes. And as the music fades and my voice rises be aware of being back here (in the classroom) and of the others around you. Gently stretch out as the music stops.

This text should be read with the voice at or just below the level of the music (see Section Five). The language is intended to be suggestive. In other words, you engage the students in asking questions for themselves. This works at an unconscious level. By saying, 'You may like to think about what makes your learning so easy?' rather than 'What makes you a good learner?' you are engaging a deep thought structure and not foreclosing on any possible answers. The guided visualization will be most successful with those who are visual learners. It helps get to a state of relaxed alertness; the optimum state for learning. It will help students experience relaxation, perhaps for the first time.

Cyclic models of learning

It would be inaccurate to suggest that there is an emerging consensus among researchers as to what produces effective learning. In his book *'Teaching Children to Learn'*, Robert Fisher compares the situation to the old story of the blind men who were holding different parts of the elephant. Each one felt a part of the animal, thinking it was the whole animal. However, practical successes with the Accelerated Learning method underwritten by new knowledge about the brain in learning suggests that a cyclic approach which accommodates a balance of input and processing styles begins to meet the success criteria of recent researchers.

Cognitive researchers, such as Dunn and Dunn, Ornstein and McCarthy emphasize the individuality of learning style preferences. Feuerstein, in attempting to separate performance from potential, has demonstrated that enrichment programmes can modify the capacity to store, organize and use information and improve learning. For Vygotsky, social interaction is the key to success in learning. The teacher extends the learners' 'zone of proximal development' – the potential for development – by encouraging paired and group work with peers and adults. Social interaction through the developing language is the medium for achieving potential.

Cyclic models describing the learning process are much favoured by learning researchers. The Accelerated Learning model is a cyclic one which accommodates the findings of the cognitive researchers on preferred learning styles. The simplest cyclic model is a plan, do, review cycle. The learner designs a solution or hypothetical solution to a problem. This is tested and the outcomes reviewed. Kolb's work on the learning cycle (1984) describes four distinct stages and suggests that the learners find some stages in the cycle more to their liking than others. This influences not only how they learn but how they prefer to pass on that learning. Kolb's stages were: concrete experience, reflective observation, abstract conceptualization and active experimentation. In this model, effective learning takes place when each stage is completed in sequence. Those who prefer the concrete experience, often described as activists, need the validation of the activity itself. Following this activity, reflectors enjoy and benefit from reviewing the experience. Theorists make conclusions based on abstract conceptualization. Pragmatists look to experiment and plan the next step.

The 4MAT Cycle devised by Bernice McCarthy in 1972 integrated an understanding of learning styles with left and right brain processing preferences. Each of four quadrants contains left and right activities and so, moving through the 4MAT Cycle, left and right brain learners access new knowledge and information more readily.

The 4MAT Cycle (diagram opposite) can be used to help plan a series of lessons around a given topic or unit of work to ensure that left and right brain learners are catered for.

McCarthy's cycle moves from concrete experience to reflective observation, to practice and personalization and finally to the integration of application and experience. The eight stages include:

1.	Creating an experience	(right brain)
2.	Reflecting, analysing the experience	(left brain)
3.	Integrating reflective analysis into concepts	(right brain)
4.	Developing concepts, skills	(left brain)
5.	Practising through 'proscribed' activity	(left brain)
6.	Practising and adding from personal experience	(right brain)
7.	Analysing, application for relevance	(left brain)
8.	Doing it and applying it to more complex situations	(right brain)

In quadrant one learners connect with what they already know. They are encouraged to pre-process the learning to come by speculating on how it will connect with what they already know. In our Accelerated Learning model this becomes the 'connection' stage. This should include activities to attach the learning to individual learner goals.

Quadrant two is the 'input' stage in our Accelerated Learning model. At this point what the learner already knows is developed through new information. The teacher provides input which is accessible to the learner.

In quadrant three, the 'activity' phase in Accelerated Learning, learners practise new skills and begin to see how they can be applied in different contexts.

Quadrant four takes practice into lifelong learning. It is here that the higher order skills of comparison, evaluation, application and prioritization are utilized to make the new skills transferable.

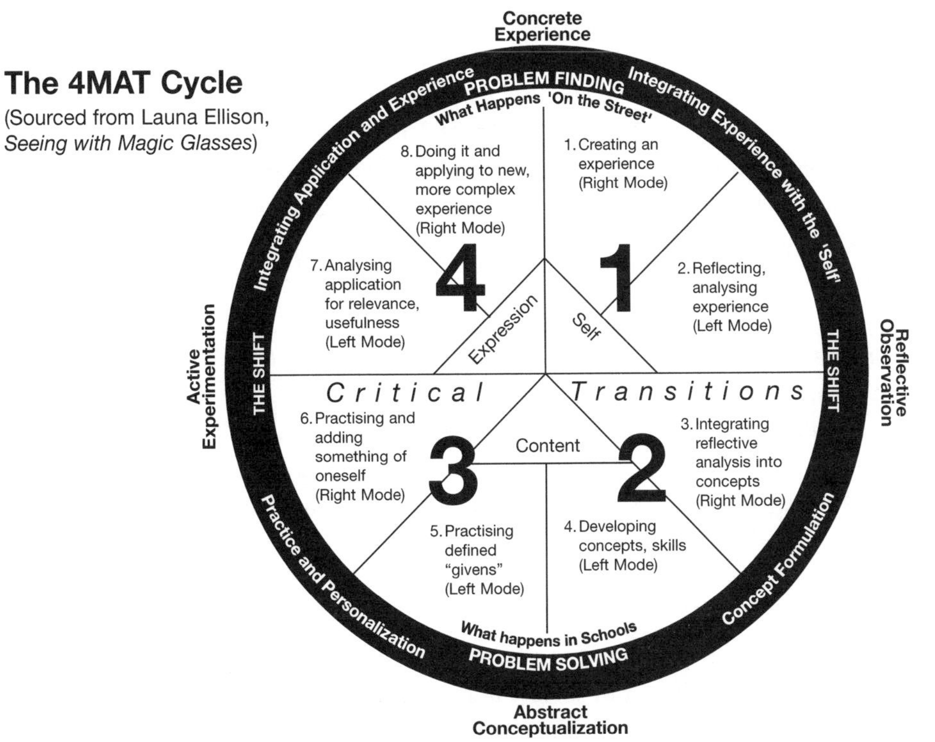

You will now appreciate that accessing the learning preferences of those in your classes requires acuity and flexibility to allow you to identify different preferences, utilize appropriate strategies and teaching tools and do so in a way which is systematic and managed. Having worked through the cycle providing input of new information via VAK, how do you ensure that you are engaging all your students in their preferred style? In the Accelerated Learning Cycle the next stage is to provide learning activities – sometimes described as activations – in the different intelligences of the learner. To do this we utilize the work on multiple intelligences developed by Howard Gardner.

Multiple Intelligences theory

'Possibly the worst educational innovation of this century was the so called intelligence test ... let us put the record straight .. we all have the ability to improve and expand our own intelligence: it is not fixed.'

Gordon Dryden and Jeannette Vos

Howard Gardner has developed a model of intelligence which has become a central part of any accelerated learning experience.

Gardner, of Harvard University, has been working on his Multiple Intelligences model for over twenty years. A genuine polymath, Gardner has drawn his evidence from neurobiology and fields such as anthropology, psychology, philosophy and history. He has published extensive studies on genius and has gathered evidence for his thesis from around the world. Building on educational theorists such as Piaget, he set out to establish that intelligence is not fixed. It is best described as a set of abilities or skills and, as such, can be developed and improved. He uses the words 'talent' and 'intelligence' interchangeably. He adds, 'There is something wrong when a person is able to do some things really very well, but is not considered smart if those things happen not to be connected to school success.'

He argues that our models of intelligence are based on concepts ultimately inherited from Alfred Binet, a French psychologist who, in 1900, was asked by the Parisian city fathers to devise a test to predict which youngsters would succeed and which would fail at primary age in French classrooms. His 'IQ' test was later adopted as a means of recruiting American soldiers for the First World War and subsequently helped contribute to current concepts of what intelligence is. For Gardner, 'IQ tests predict school peformance with considerable accuracy but they are only an indifferent predictor of performance in a profession after formal schooling.' Whole generations of teachers have, and continue to, pigeonhole youngsters on the basis of such 'intelligence' tests.

> ***People like me are aware of their so-called genius at eight, nine, ten ... I always wondered, 'Why has nobody discovered me? In school, didn't they see that I'm more clever than anybody in this school? That the teachers are stupid, too? That all they had was information I didn't need.' It was obvious to me. Why didn't they put me into art school? Why didn't they train me? I was different, I was always different. Why didn't anybody notice me?***
>
> John Lennon

Gardner's view of intelligence is that it is a human intellectual competence that 'enables one to solve problems encountered in society and to create effective products'. It also entails the potential for finding or creating problems, thereby laying the groundwork for the acquisition of new knowledge. For Gardner, a human intelligence emerges only in an appropriate cultural context: 'The ideal of what is valued will differ markedly, sometimes even radically, across human cultures.'

Gardner's seven intelligences are groupings of abilities or skills and not absolute quantities.

He describes the intelligences as:

1. **Linguistic:** a facility with language, patterning and systems.

2. **Mathematical and logical**: likes precision and enjoys abstract and structured thinking.

3. **Visual and spatial:** thinks in pictures and mental images, good with maps, charts and diagrams, uses movement to assist learning.

4. **Musical:** sensitive to mood and emotion, enjoys rhythm, understands complex organization of music.

5. **Interpersonal:** relates well to others, mediator, good communicator.

6. **Intrapersonal:** self motivated, high degree of self-knowledge, strong sense of values.

7. **Kinesthetic:** good timing, skilled at handicrafts, likes to act and touch, good control of objects.

Work completed by others in the field of accelerated learning suggests that the development of a full range of intelligences assists long-term learning generally. Effective teaching will provide learning opportunities for a range of intelligences.

In the United Kingdom we have tended to value what we can assess rather than assess what we value.

This means that the left-brain abilities which comprise part of those intelligences Gardner has described as linguistic and as mathematical/logical, are increasingly recognized and validated as students get older. The hidden curriculum revolves around social status, so 'interpersonal intelligence is rewarded with friendship or leadership roles'. The intrapersonal intelligence is the most neglected. Children are, 'left to develop it for themselves because there is almost no help from schools'. This is particularly evident in boys. Recent studies on underachievement in boys point up the lack of opportunity for boys to be open about, to explore and to share their feelings. This, in turn, leads to an underdevelopment of their own 'affective' potential which is compounded by systems which don't teach to the intrapersonal intelligence.

Funding difficulties have sometimes led to extra-curricular activity – dance, music, sports, drama – being less accessible for some children in our schools. This means that the bodily/kinesthetic, musical and visual/spatial intelligences are provided with fewer formal opportunities for expression.

Most learners will have a 'jagged' profile. This means that they will be high in some areas and low in others. There are no particular pattern of intelligences which tend to develop together or be disassociated from one another. Gardner describes them as 'semi-autonomous' and adds that there are no neurological reasons why any combination of intelligences can't be developed together.

Tony Buzan's early work reiterated the view of many pioneering neuro-scientists that development of one half of the brain produces a corresponding development in those functions controlled by the other half. Gardner believes that each intelligence is modifiable and can be expanded. There are predictable factors such as cultural influences in and around the home. As the senses are activated and cellular connections are made throughout childhood, so the intelligence is developed. The more stimulation the more the development. For Gardner, each of us may be born with all the intelligences but some develop slightly, some strongly and others hardly at all. To access each of the seven intelligences we must first understand what each comprises.

Linguistic

It is likely that a person with a well developed linguistic intelligence will ...

- *learn through listening, writing, reading and discussing*
- *be responsive to the potential of the written and spoken word to persuade, amuse, convey information, construct meaning and entertain*
- *imitate or mimic the linguistic idiosyncrasies of others*
- *be enthused about developing their own application and understanding of language*
- *be a better than average communicator in written and spoken modes and be an attentive listener*
- *have a predominantly auditory representational system*

Linguistic ability may express itself and be valued differently in different cultures. For example, writing ability in one culture, story-telling through song, poetry or prose in another culture or an ability to manipulate language through puzzles or anagrams in a third.

Linguistic intelligence is universal. A specific part of the brain – Broca's area – is responsible for the production of grammatical sentences. Children across the world share a remarkable similarity in their acquisition of language. It is adults who designate a spoken language to be more easy or more difficult to learn than another. A baby doesn't decide to pop back into its mother's womb on discovering that he or she is expected to learn Mandarin Chinese! Lozanov recognized that, for language learning, an environment with no risk of failure which is fun, experimental and challenging, succesfully simulates the childhood conditions where one's facility for language learning is at its peak. His suggestopaedic language classes succeed because he reproduces these conditions in an environment where it is consistently 'suggested' through spoken language patterns, classroom environment and the non-verbal communication of the teacher that participants will learn.

Linguistic intelligence includes a sensitivity to the meaning of words, to their order, to the sounds, rhythm and inflection of words and their capacity to change mood, persuade or convey information.

A learner with a linguistic intelligence in your classroom will display a fascination for words and their manipulation. He or she will love puns, poems, rhymes, 'plays on words', expressing themselves on paper and/or orally and listening to stories.

Mathematical and Logical

A learner who has a well developed mathematical and logical intelligence will ...

- *demonstrate an ability to understand and manipulate abstract symbols to represent concrete objects and concepts*

Individuals with a mathematical and logical intelligence are problem solvers who can construct solutions non-verbally. They delight in sequence, logic and order. They can discern patterns and relationships and are capable of deductive and inductive reasoning.

Gardner views Piaget's model of cognitive development as largely a description of the development of the mathematical and logical intelligence. So, from the child's interaction with objects in space and time, through the discovery of number and a growing understanding of abstract symbolism and an ability to manipulate such symbols, to the sophisticated ability to recognize the implications of hypotheses, we

have a description of the evolution of the mathematical and logical intelligence.
A learner with a mathematical and logical intelligence in your classroom will enjoy solutions and take delight in syllogisms and analogies. He or she will also enjoy finding and using codes. These could be symbolic, alphabetical or numerical. They may also enjoy sequencing activities, work with number, measurement and estimation. A mathematical and logical intelligence can be displayed in all disciplines across the curriculum.

- *be familiar at an early stage with the concepts of time, space, quantity, number and cause and effect*
- *be good at solving logical puzzles and working out sequence*
- *discern the pattern in relationships*
- *be capable of mathematical thinking: for example, formulate arguments based on hard data, gather evidence, estimate, build models and make hypotheses*
- *seek to find harmony and order in his or her environment*

Visual and Spatial

A chess-player, a navigator and an interior designer all exhibit visual and spatial intelligence. Spatial problem solving involves visualizing an object seen from a different angle perhaps manipulating it in three dimensions and through space and time. The right hemisphere of the brain controls these functions. An individual with damage to the right side of the brain often loses the ability to recognize faces or scenes, to manoeuvre around objects or find a way around sites. Sometimes they may also find difficulty in envisaging a mental image.

A visual and spatial intelligence is highly evident in childhood. Often our capacity to create vivid mental pictures, and to use our imaginations to daydream, diminishes as we grow older and we are discouraged from such activities. Thinking in images is easier for some than others. However, we can relearn this skill in a positive and useful way. Research has shown that developing the ability to create mental images involves an 'activation of latent electro-chemical circuitry in the brain' and that, 'the image of an imagined object or situation has mental effects that are in some ways very similar to the image of an object that is actually perceived ... if one is able to imagine something to be true, part of the mind appears to accept that imagined outcome as reality.'

A learner with visual and spatial intelligence will ...

- *be able to visualize easily and imagine scenes readily*
- *be good at manoeuvring when this involves manipulating self or body through space*
- *be able to construct, build or conceive three-dimensional objects or imagine their 'unfolded' construction*
- *know the effect that the movement of gears or pulleys have on other things around them*
- *learn through seeing and observing and be able to memory map*
- *anticipate the movement of an object – such as a ball – in space*
- *have a talent for interpreting and constructing graphs, maps or other visual media*

Those with a developed visual and spatial intelligence are naturally able to re-create images of scenes or objects and therefore the emotional associations that they carry with them. This equips them with a potential for creativity often missing to others.

Visual problem-solving tools such as series of events chains, force-field analysis, topic webs, spider diagrams and memory maps will access the visual and spatial intelligence of those learners in your class. The visual and spatial skills required to interpret the work of Dali and Escher will be easier for these learners than others. The use of peripherals placed at or higher than eye level will have significant impact on the visual and spatial learner: make them bright and colourful with varying shapes. Rotate the seating arrangements from time to time in your class. This changes the perspective on the visual stimuli you provide.

Musical

A learner with musical intelligence will show some ability to ...

- *discern pattern in sounds and enjoy experimenting with them*
- *show sensitivity to mood changes in sounds and be able to pick out individual instruments*
- *be susceptible to changes in their own state as a result of listening to music*
- *enjoy improvising and playing with sounds of different sorts*
- *show an interest and some facility for playing a musical instrument*
- *have a sense of ryhthm and be able to respond to music by dance or drama or composing*
- *be curious about music and seek to develop their own categories and preferences*

Acording to Gardner, evidence from child prodigies supports the claim that there is a biological link to a particular intelligence. Musical talent emerges very early. Yehudi Menuhin was an international performer at the age of three. The right brain controls the perception and production of music. For many musicians tones, rhythms and larger musical patterns are constantly in their consciousness. Composers constantly work and re-work these patterns. Nancy Ellis, Principal of the Simon Guggenheim School on the South side of Chicago, describes how many of her middle-school students can 'rap' all day remembering the lyrics with exact recall and constructing new and imaginative ones but are often unable – without music – to recall the key points of a short piece of prose.

The students in the Hungarian singing schools of Zoltan Kodaly also show excellence in maths and science. Many researchers attribute this to skills developed in manipulating pitch, tone, timbre and rhythm and understanding the relationships of the unique notating symbol systems from the earliest age. Musical intelligence does not necessarily mean an ability in composing and playing music. Nor does it necessitate an ability to read music. When 17 countries were surveyed for the science achievements of 14 year olds one of the common characteristics of the top three – Holland, Japan and Hungary – was the extent of intensive music and art training in their state schools.

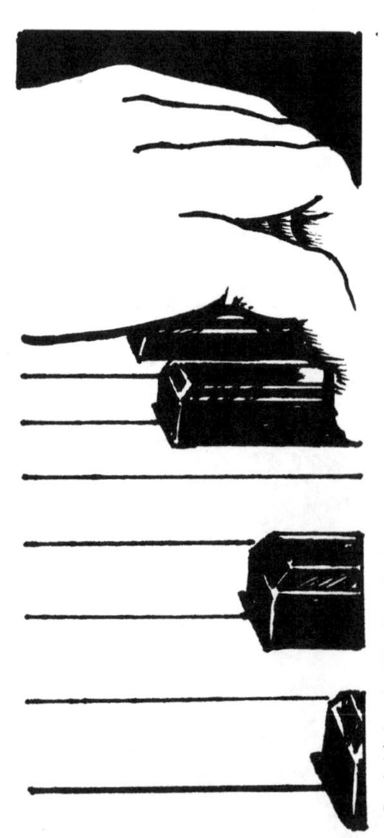

Music in the classroom can create mood, break-states and separate out learning sessions. It can create an atmosphere of relaxed alertness which is conducive to learning. It can be used to energize or relax.

A learner with musical intelligence in your classroom will enjoy singing and the rhythms and rhymes of songs, poems, jingles, raps, choral readings and nonsense sounds. They may learn well by recording their own learning to music or constructing raps or jingles which summarize the key learning. A set of historical dates, mathematical formulae or the elements of the periodic table rapped or sung to a powerful beat will stay in the memory longer than the familiar, if dulcet, tones of the teacher!

Interpersonal

Gardner believes the 'personal' intelligences – interpersonal and intrapersonal – tend to use all other forms of intelligence in their operation.

Interpersonal intelligence is an ability to enter into the 'map' of another. To begin to make sense of the world from another's viewpoint. To adjust one's behaviour accordingly. The interpersonal intelligence allows the observation of subtle changes of mood and behaviour, motivation and intention. It is highly developed in successful, therapists, teachers, counsellors and sales people. According to Gardner, 'Intelligence builds upon a core capacity to notice distinctions among others.'

A learner with well-developed interpersonal intelligence will enjoy paired and small group activities and collaborative learning. They will also enjoy exercises which require looking at issues from a number of human perspectives, empathizing, devising class rules – agreeing roles and responsibilities, interviewing adults other than teachers and participating in conflict management games.

The interpersonal intelligence expresses itself through an ability to ...

- *see issues from diverse perspectives*
- *form, build and maintain a variety of social relationships with others*
- *know and understand the thoughts, feelings, attitudes and behaviours of others*
- *work in teams and contribute to their positive dynamic*
- *communicate effectively verbally and non-verbally*
- *listen, acknowledge and respond to the views of others*
- *influence others*

Intrapersonal

Whereas interpersonal intelligence is largely concerned with others, intrapersonal intelligence is concerned with knowledge about and identity of the self. The intrapersonal intelligence is self-knowledge. It denotes the ability to access one's own feelings and emotions, to judge and make sense of them with some discrimination and then to draw some conclusions about them which will guide subsequent behaviour. The more we are able to bring our inner feelings and emotions to consciousness, the better we can relate our outer world to the world of everyday experience. Those with a strong intrapersonal intelligence will be self-motivated, have a high degree of self-knowledge and a strong sense of values.

NLP has provided us with many tools for interrupting and changing unhelpful patterns of intrapersonal thinking. Some of these techniques are described in detail elsewhere in this book. Research into thinking about thinking - metacognition - has discovered countless strategies for improving our thinking patterns and teaching others to do the same. Feuerstein's work on instrumental enrichment outlines a methodology for developing thinking skills.

Those with a developed intrapersonal intelligence will:

- *be aware of their thoughts, feelings and emotions and seek explanations for them*
- *attempt to find solutions to philosophical questions*
- *have an accurate picture of themselves*

☛ *be consistent in living to and applying a set of personal values and beliefs*
☛ *value personal growth and development*
☛ *be self-motivated*
☛ *enjoy quiet reflection time*
☛ *utilize journals and diaries*

The well-developed intrapersonal ability will be apparent in learners who utilize journals and diaries to assist their learning and who are able to work independently. Sometimes introverted or shy, the intrapersonal learner will test their learning against strongly held personal convictions. In class or group discussion the intrapersonal learner will take up considered positions and particularly enjoy discussing the 'big' issues. While they may have a clarity about personal goals it might be at the expense of more pragmatic considerations.

Many boys have an underdeveloped intrapersonal ability. Boys, being later developers linguistically, grow up with an emphasis on doing rather than talking. It is often the case that they are not encouraged to discuss and be open about feelings or to develop a vocabulary to articulate those feelings. Boys are less reflective than girls at an early age. Their world is more likely to be hierarchical, action-focused and competitive. To develop the intrapersonal intelligence of boys you should also:

- ☛ reinforce basic reading and literacy skills especially using diaries and other reflective tools
- ☛ ask questions and encourage the use of a wide register of affective language
- ☛ in team-working emphasize collaborative problem solving rather than competition
- ☛ structure discussion activity in pairs and fours
- ☛ positive stroke for accuracy and neatness, openness and reflection
- ☛ utilize lots of beginnings and endings and chunk down content
- ☛ utilize guided visualizations using relaxation techniques to appropriate music
- ☛ build a consistent reward system on BASIS principles

Kinesthetic

The kinesthetic or bodily-kinesthetic intelligence is characterized by the ability to use one's body in highly differentiated and skilled ways; to work skilfully with objects and manipulate them with finesse. Highly developed kinesthetic intelligence is apparent in dancers, athletes, sculptors, model makers, actors, machinists, jewellers and perhaps even the fish filleter! NLP training talks about getting a new skill 'into the muscle'. Certainly physical movement aids memory by 'encoding learning experiences into the neuro-musculature'. We often learn by doing. The student who is unable to remember the relative position of the countries of the world from the school atlas will often remember when they are painted out onto the playground and he or she is asked to move between them. Similarly, the electronics engineering student who has difficulty describing circuitry on paper can often make you a sophisticated circuit board effortlessly. As students grow older and progress through school the opportunities for kinesthetic learning sadly become fewer.

A kinesthetic learner in your classroom will be accessed through simulations and role play, drama, mime, body sculptures, break-states and energizers, field trips and visits. The kinesthetic learner will enjoy rummaging in resource boxes and doing group games which involve floor movements.

A developed kinesthetic intelligence is exhibited by...

- ***exploring through touch, movement, manipulation and physical experience***
- ***learning by doing***
- ***enjoyment of field trips, model building, role play, video production, collections***
- ***co-ordination, sense of timing and balance, dexterity, grace***
- ***concern over improvement in physical performance; rehearses movement***
- ***demonstrating creativity through physical movement and expression***
- ***often restless***

The Multiple Intelligences questionnaire
The Multiple Intelligences questionnaire is a quick way of assessing the balance of intelligences among the students in your class. It can be used as a resource for work on ability and potential.

Multiple Intelligences questionnaire

Complete the questionnaire on the following page by assigning a numerical value to each of the statements which you consider represent you. If you agree that the statement very strongly represents you, assign a 5. If the statement does not represent you, assign a 0. Use the numbers 5 – 0 to grade each statement.

1. I am skilful in working with objects ....

2. I have a good sense of direction ....

3. I have a natural ability to sort out arguments between friends ....

4. I can remember the words to music easily ....

5. I am able to explain topics which are difficult and make them clear ....

6. I alway do things one step at a time ....

7. I know myself well and understand why I behave as I do ....

8. I enjoy community activities and social events ....

9. I learn well from talks, lectures and listening to others ....

10. When listening to music I experience changes in mood ....

11. I enjoy puzzles, crosswords, logical problems ....

12. Charts, diagrams, visual displays are important for my learning ....

13 I am sensitive to the moods and feelings of those around me ....

14 I learn best when I have to get up and do it for myself ....

15 I need to see something in it for me before I want to learn something ....

16 I like privacy and quiet for working and thinking ....

17 I can pick out individual instruments in complex musical pieces ....

18 I can visualize remembered and constructed scenes easily ....

19 I have a well developed vocabulary and am expressive with it ....

20 I enjoy and value taking written notes ....

21 I have a good sense of balance and enjoy physical movement ....

22 I can discern pattern and relationships between experiences or things ....

23 In teams I co-operate and build on the ideas of others ....

24 I am observant and will often see things others miss ....

25 I get restless easily ....

26 I enjoy working or learning independently of others ....

27 I enjoy making music ....

28 I have a facility with numbers and mathematical problems ....

Now transfer the outcomes to the list of seven intelligences on the page opposite and then complete the sectioned wheel.

Multiple Intelligences: key to statements

Intelligence		Statements	Total score
Linguistic		5 9 19 20	
	scoring	....	....
Mathematical and logical		6 11 22 28	
	scoring	....	....
Visual and spatial		2 12 18 24	
	scoring	....	....
Musical		4 10 17 27	
	scoring	....	....
Interpersonal		3 8 13 23	
	scoring	....	....
Intrapersonal		7 15 16 26	
	scoring	....	....
Kinesthetic		1 14 21 25	
	scoring	....	....

Multiple Intelligences wheel

By taking the total numerical score against each intelligence from the questionnaire, plotting it on the wheel and shading each segment you will get a visual representation of your balance of intelligences according to Howard Gardner's theory.

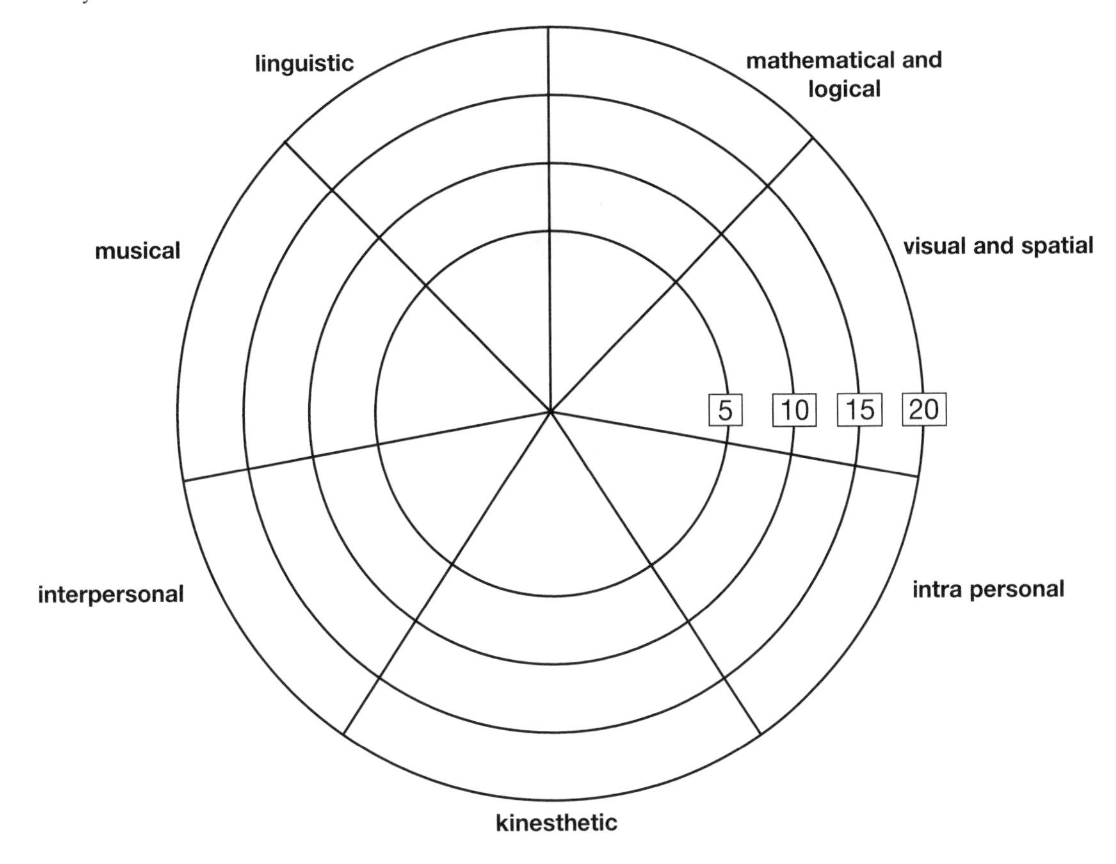

The significance of the Accelerated Learning Cycle

The Accelerated Learning Cycle has evolved from an understanding of how the brain operates in learning, how learners can be motivated and helped to believe they can achieve, awareness of representational systems and the adoption of multiple intelligences theory. Its seven stages can and ought to be moved through very quickly. Content is delivered via all the processes. Profound learning is taking place at each stage. By using the techniques described in this book the learners are themselves empowered at each stage in the cycle. For example, in stage one, 'connecting the learning', you can use memory mapping techniques to initiate thinking about a new topic. Each individual begins his or her map on what is already known, then compares in a pair and then in a four. Immediately you've initiated some learning of content, encouraged the asking of key questions and begun to stimulate problem solving. You describe the Big Picture in stage two and in stage three 'outcomes' can once again be initiated by students using simple techniques such as, 'In pairs agree three things you'd like to be able to do or know by the end of this lesson' or, 'For this to be the most useful lesson you've ever had agree three things you would want.' Stages six and seven lend themselves very well to a variety of student-centred approaches using the techniques described in this book.

The Accelerated Learning Cycle described here has seven stages. Each stage and its place in the cycle is of equal importance. A further pre-stage – the supportive learning environment – is a constant, and operates like a guide-rail keeping the Accelerated Learning Cycle running true.

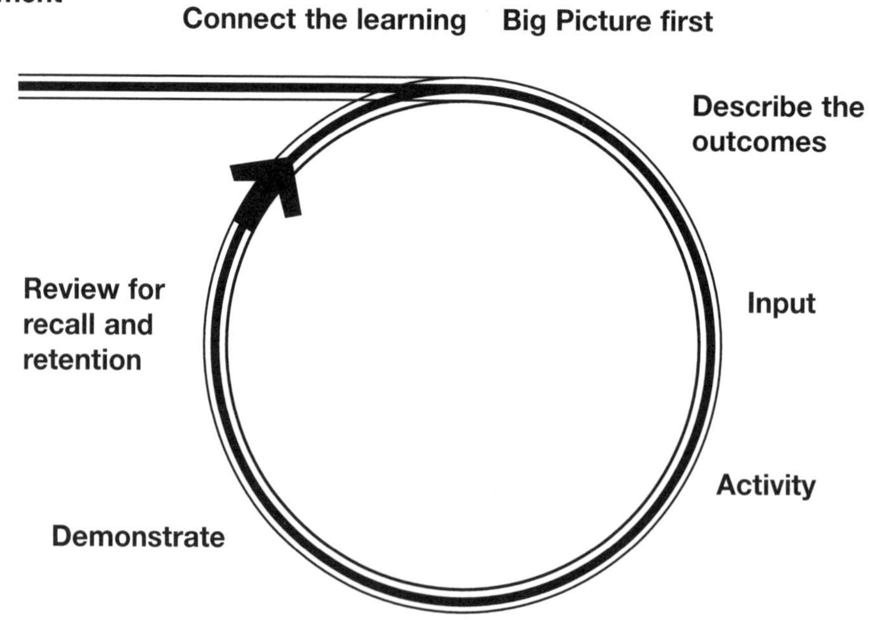

Some of the interventions one might expect to see at each stage of the cycle are outlined on the following pages.

The Accelerated Learning Cycle looks like this...

Pre-Stage

Create the supportive learning environment

This is the pre-stage where the right conditions for learning have to be in place.

- ☞ the learner must be free from anxiety or stress and be challenged
- ☞ use energizers or relaxers to access the most receptive state of mind
- ☞ the elements of BASIS are in place
- ☞ the teacher communicates high expectations positively

Stage One

Connect the learning

This is the stage where the topic or unit of work is connected with what has gone before and what is to come.

- ☞ assist the learner to connect to his or her long-term goals
- ☞ help learners understand their learning strengths and preferred styles
- ☞ help learners see how this follows previous work and anticipates what is to come
- ☞ use prediction exercises to access what is already known and to preprocess thinking about the content to come

Stage Two

Big Picture

Describe the content of the lesson first.

- ☞ access right-brain learners
- ☞ continue preprocessing the questions learners will have begun to ask themselves
- ☞ begin to alleviate anxieties over the accessibility and relevance of the material

Stage Three

Describes the outcomes

Tell the students what they will have achieved by the end of the lesson or invite them to set their own outcomes

- ☞ chunk down the content into bite-sized pieces
- ☞ use positive language, 'By the end of this lesson you will have...'
- ☞ differentiate outcomes using must, should, could...

Stage Four

Input

Input the content of the lesson, topic or unit utilizing VAK.

- ☞ the input of new information should utilize Visual, Auditory and Kinesthetic modes
- ☞ the input stage can access the long-term memory if sufficiently

memorable – see SCOTS CLAN MAPS (on pages 82–83)

- ☞ input can be repeated using different strategies, for example, active concert, dramatized reading, visual display
- ☞ the duration of the input stage should not exceed the on task capability of the learner

Stage Five
Activity

Utilize the balance of multiple intelligences in your learning by designing appropriate activities to access the content.

- ☞ access all seven of the multiple intelligences
- ☞ provide a 'balanced diet' of activities (over time)
- ☞ encourage them to know and use the learning cycle
- ☞ use individual, pair and group activity
- ☞ encourage learners to make choices and set success criteria

Stage Six
Demonstrate

In this stage the learners demonstrate their understanding of the new knowledge.

- ☞ use paired 'shares' with memory maps, posters, booklets, visual displays and other ways of 'showing you know'
- ☞ demonstrations, tests, quizzes, talks, mock lessons
- ☞ encouraging reflection on processes used
- ☞ provide opportunities to 'model' success (see Section Seven)

Stage Seven
Review for recall and retention

Review is vital to long-term learning and recall.

- ☞ use a variety of review techniques (see Section Four)
- ☞ teach different memory and recall techniques
- ☞ concert review
- ☞ utilize the active listening approach

In Accelerated Learning we move the learner through the cycle quickly ensuring throughout that the 'guide-rail' of the supportive learning environment is in place.

Memory Map of models of learning

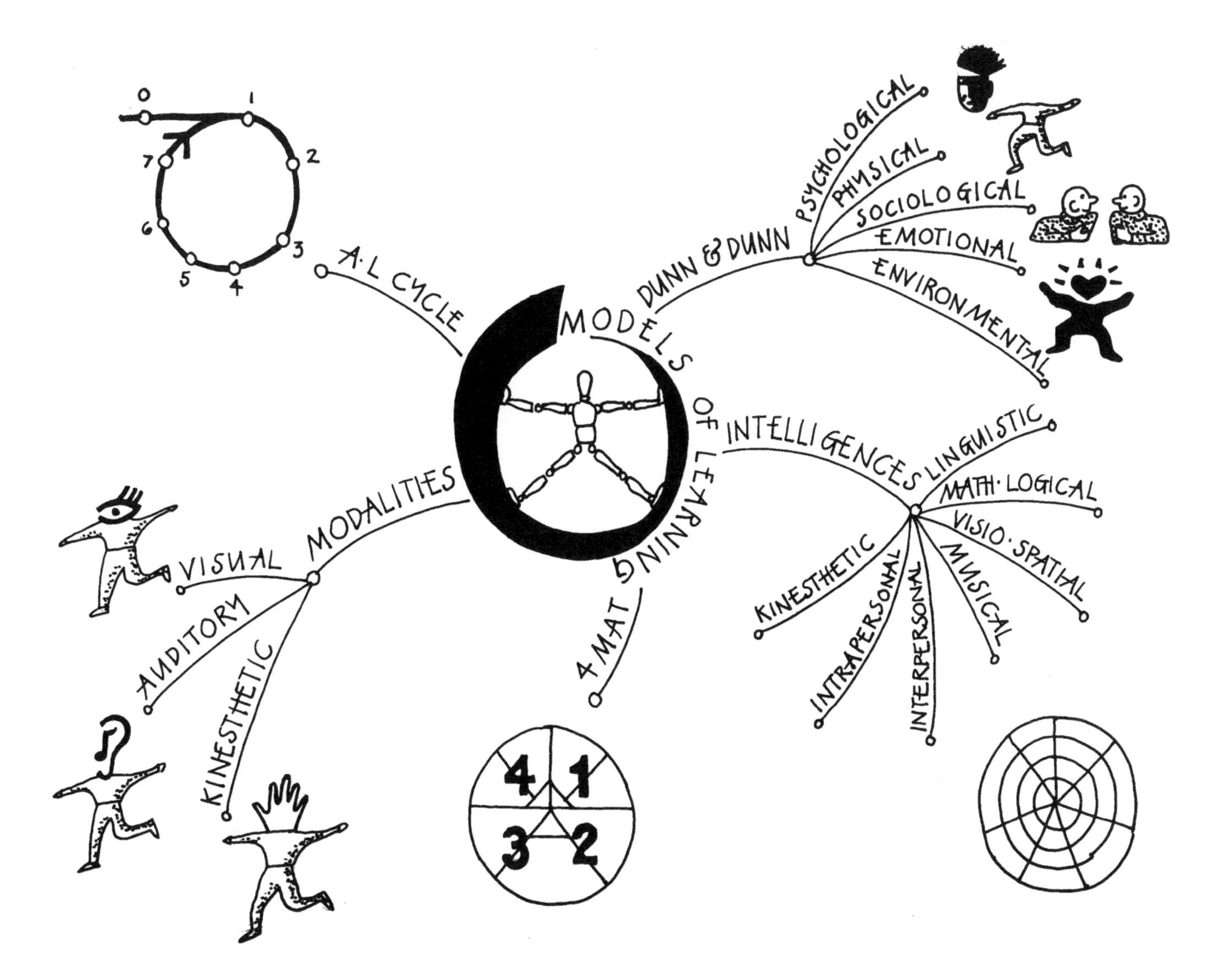

Review

Key questions about models of learning

- what factors influence learning style?
- what practical steps can you take to help students better understand their preferred learning styles?
- in what ways is each stage of the Accelerated Learning Cycle important?
- how does VAK contribute to whole brain learning?
- describe learners whom you know who match each of the seven intelligences?
- what classroom activities can you use in your subject to develop each of the seven intelligences?

The learning environment

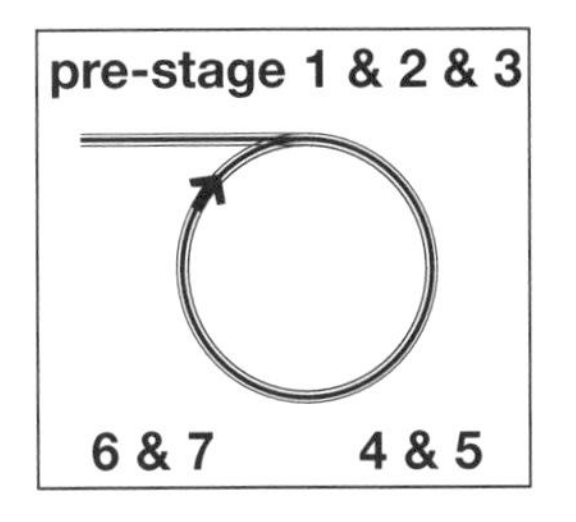

In Section Four you will learn how ...

- ***to improve on classroom layout***
- ***the best learning environment is one of high challenge and low stress***
- ***ritualized and patterned positive teacher behaviour influences performance***
- ***constant and varied exposure to new material encourages quicker and deeper learning***
- ***differentiated structures are necessary for effective individualized learning***
- ***to use break-states, energisers and relaxers***
- ***music can be used to improve recall as well as to create the learning environment of your choice***

The learning environment

Teaching and learning are not coterminous. Energetic and conscientious teaching can produce little or no learning. Similarly, learning can take place with little or no teaching. Once we understand this we have a choice. This is the difference between the effective teacher and the ineffective. An effective teacher chooses teaching methods and organizational strategies to meet the needs of the learners. He or she designs the learning environment, where practical, to help deliver the objectives of the lesson.

The teacher is not the main event as far as learners are concerned! Their learning is taking place at all times when they are in the school. It may not be the learning which the school seeks. It may run counter to what the school espouses, but it occurs nevertheless. That is why the learning environment should be just that – that is, an environment which promotes learning.

School buildings and their layout, classroom shape and size, furniture, heating and lighting all impact on learning. In nearly every case they also happen to be the things you can do little to change for the better. You inherit the physical circumstances in which you work. However, improvements, if limited, are always possible.

Eric Jensen, in his book, *SuperTeaching*, states that the use of positive visual reinforcement of key learning points through posters or peripherals placed at or above eye level around the classroom improves long-term recall by as much as 90 per cent. As a callow youth I can remember learning Latin vocabulary by writing it out onto the back of a large poster, pinning it to the wall, lying on my bed and reading it. Visual reinforcement of key learning points, affirming statements, posters of positive role models and student's work – carefully presented and changed every 2–4 weeks – will, when placed at eye level or above, improve the quality of learning in your classroom.

If you do not have quality display space in your classroom try to persuade your school to make it a priority. Large, wooden-framed display boards screwed to the wall at eye level and above are ideal. If you don't have your own classroom then perhaps the next best thing is to laminate some of your key display material. Printers can provide this service up to A1 (flip chart size) for a reasonable charge.

The worst room layout is one where desks are fixed and in rows and where movement between or around is inhibited by lack of space. Obstructions made by bags, coats, hockey sticks, skateboards, and any of the other things students carry with them; will further impede movement and make your classroom management less flexible. If possible, agree protocols about storing bags and coats with your classes: make their storage part of the ritual you build around welcoming. Desks in rows limit the opportunities for small group work and for moving students around the class as part of your learning activities. The best classroom arrangements allow for flexibility. If possible, your layout should allow easy movement between groups, a focal area for formal presentation and for some larger group activities or for kinesthetic work, resource spaces in each corner and good sight lines both for you and for your students.

Avoid the T Spot phenomenon! The **T Spot** is the front row of desks and those on either side of an avenue down the centre. Students sitting in these places get more attention from the teacher. Other phenomena to be aware of are the **Halo effect** – focusing more attention on brighter, more able and more 'attractive' students and the **Pareto effect** – 20 per cent of the students occupying 80 per cent of your time. Catch yourself every now and again and review who, specifically, you are engaging with and how, and this can be avoided. The easiest way is, however, to manage the physical aspects of your class.

Make moving around a key process in learning. As part of your classroom management resource you should record and display different groupings of, say fours, for each class and display these. Each group of desks should also have a number, letter or name. Eight different combinations of groups (of say four) would allow you to manage your mix of learners.

Rotate them regularly with minimal fuss and allow them to develop different sorts of relationships. Moving around the room changes your perspective on what is happening. One thing that saddens me about my short career as a schoolboy Latin scholar is that, apart from drawing coloured cross-sections of Roman walls, roads and aqueducts, my strongest memory is of the desk that I sat at for two years!

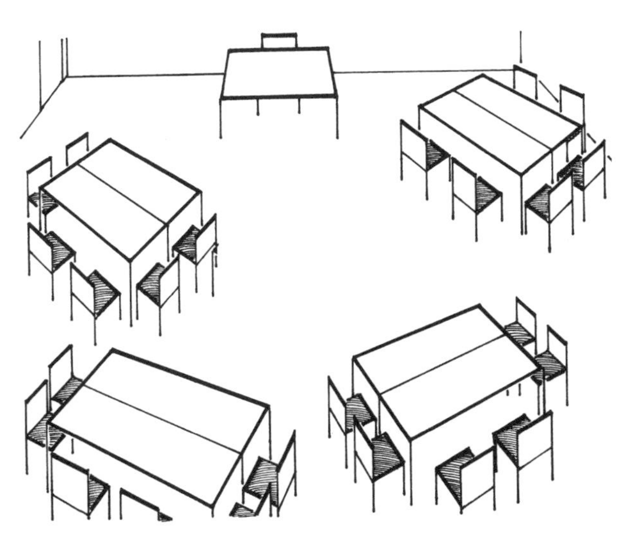

The best classroom I have visited recently was a geography class where it was evident on walking through the door that the teacher took a pride in her subject, her relationship with the learners and in the appearance of the class. Bright visual displays of work were placed alongside large posters of beautiful scenery. There was a subject bulletin board with interesting snippets of information and an affirmation wall where individual bricks comprised students' statements about what they liked about geography. On another board behind the teacher's desk were photographs of the most recent field trip. Lots of trailing plants, strategically and safely placed, added to a sense of calm. As a learning environment it gave out positive messages: the subject is significant, accessible and enjoyable; we take pride in our learning; we value each other.

The reptilian brain is responsible for ritual behaviours. Rituals, properly conducted, as part of learning can reduce learner stress. Improperly conducted, they can be a major source of stress. Different sorts of rituals can be used to enrich and support the learning experience. We all seek, enjoy and benefit from positive ritual. Here are a few which will improve the learning in your classes.

Welcoming

Be at the door to greet students. Be welcoming and positive!

You may not have time to speak to each student but over time do notice something positive about each of them. Remember names and use them. Use the chained technique to help younger students learn each others' names - for example, 'I'm ... Alert Alistair, Brave Barbara, Clever Colin ..'

Use the different review techniques as part of registering - for example, 'Alistair' followed by a keyword from the last lesson.

Expectations

Set out the Big Picture by connecting what's to come with what went before.

Relax students by working on relaxation techniques, 'Hands up everyone who's ready to learn today?' and be positive, 'Hands up everyone who's feeling positive?'

'Take a deep breath ... do it three times ... if you're ready to learn let it out!'

Previewing

Describe what they will have achieved by the end of the lesson. Write it in the corner of the board.

Do a 'paired share' on what they will have done by the end of the lesson.

After paired shares take the new information to fours. Each student explains what the other hopes to get out of the lesson. Spend no more than three minutes on both stages.

Break-states

Drum rolls! Announce Brain Gym® or partner changes or the introduction of a key revision point with a 'drum roll'. To do a drum roll students smack both hands quickly on the desk or on their knees. You stop it by conducting with an imaginary baton! Remember the 'on-task' times and include break-states as part of each lesson.

Celebrations

Catch each student being successful at least once and let everyone else know. Organize activities where pairs describe one thing they've done well or are proud of or are good at or they discovered about themselves. Ask the students for immediate feedback. For example, 'Hands up with marks out of five (fingers) if you've understood that last point. Turn to the person next to you and explain your mark.'

Closing lessons

Practise relaxers, visualizations and short review activities. Review the content of the lesson while the students relax, 'In groups share three positive things you've learned today.'

You must not expect to disappear into a telephone box, whirl around, and come back out with 'Superteacher' written across your chest! These rituals are only rituals if they are part of your regular repertoire. Practise them and develop them over time. Engage your colleagues in what you are doing. Explain it to them and to the students.

Break-states and Brain Gym® for managing the energy levels of your class

Brain Gym® is a quick and effective way of changing the physical and mental state of the learners in your class. It involves physical and mental activity. It connects left and right brain and it helps improve motor co-ordination.

It can be used at the beginning or end of lessons or topics. It is safe, enjoyable and non-threatening. There is a great deal of research into kinesiology which suggests that regular use of the Brain Gym® activities can alleviate stress, improve hand-eye co-ordination, improve the concentration on focused activities and quicken the response times to visual stimuli. If you have encountered the Alexander Technique you may be familiar with some of these activities.

Explain the purpose to the students in your class. Encourage them to practise at home and perhaps teach their parents, brothers and sisters. Do make sure that some of the more physical co-ordinating activities are within the capability of all those in your class.

Double doodle

On a large sheet of paper draw large, continuous and overlapping mirror shapes using both hands simultaneously. Use felt pens and continue to draw in easy looped movements. Begin with large simple shapes like circles, eights, squares or triangles. Be aware of the mirrored movements and graduate to more detailed drawing.

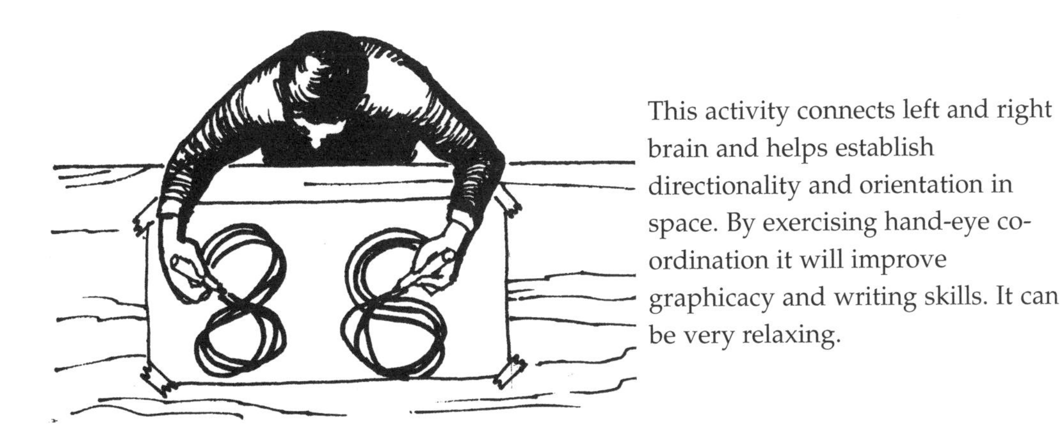

This activity connects left and right brain and helps establish directionality and orientation in space. By exercising hand-eye co-ordination it will improve graphicacy and writing skills. It can be very relaxing.

Names in the air

With your preferred hand write out your full name in the air. Use large movements. Do it forwards and backwards. Now use your other hand to write your name with both hands simultaneously. If you are right-handed, start in the centre and work out. If you are left-handed start at the outside and work in. Try this several times before going on to another name. You can also do this activity in class with keywords which you are about to use or with 'difficult' spellings or with numbers or formulae.

Another left and right brain activity which helps establish directionality and orientation in space. It can be a fun way of practising spelling, previewing or reviewing keywords or team-building. As an exercise, 'names in the air' can be used to help make difficult spellings memorable. Have the student practise it with each hand then both hands and then on successful completion place the drawn image in their upper left field of vision. Ask them to write it in the air again but this time with their eyes closed.

Lazy eights

With one arm extended in front of you and your thumb pointing upwards trace the shape of a figure eight in the air. The eight should be on its side and as you trace it out in large, slow movements focus your eyes on your thumb. Without moving your head trace three eights in successively larger movements. Now do it with your other hand and then clasp them together and do both.

Before and after research shows that binocular and peipheral vision improve after lazy eights. The activity connects right and left visual fields and improves balance and co-ordination.

Lazy elephants
With the same movements and benefits as lazy eights, the elephant involves tracing eights by placing your head on your shoulder and looking along your extended arm. Focus beyond your hand and lean gently forward. The elephant helps to relax tension in the neck.

Rub a dubs
Gently rub your hand in a circle on your tummy. Stop, then pat your head with your other hand gently. Now do both at the same time and at a similar pace. You should be rubbing your tummy while patting your head. Try to maintain the difference in each movement. Swop around. Pat your tummy while rubbing your head. This activity connects left and right brain and is pure fun! It helps co-ordination. It focuses attention and can take your mind 'off' whatever was preoccupying it beforehand.

'This and that'
Verbal instructions – 'do this' or 'do that' – accompany physical actions which your students have to emulate or not. If your instruction is 'do this' the students mimic your physical action. If your instruction is 'do that' the students avoid mimicking your physical action and continue as before. A simple break-state activity which helps develop listening skills.

Cross crawl
Standing begin to 'march' in time. Raise your knees and alternately touch each knee with your opposite hand. Progressively, move your elbows to each knee in sequence. An alternative is to touch each heel behind your back with opposite hands.

Cross crawl activates both halves of the brain together. Research suggests that it improves co-ordination, visual, auditory and kinesthetic ability and can improve listening, writing and memory.

Alphabet edit
Alphabet edit is a challenge. It is a very useful activity for clearing the mind of any baggage brought to the classroom and which may be getting in the way of learning. It involves reading aloud the letters of the alphabet in sequence beginning to end or end to beginning. It can be used for practising spelling and for learning the alphabet.

A	B	C	D	E	F	G
l	t	r	r	t	t	l
H	I	J	K	L	M	N
l	r	t	t	r	l	l
O	P	Q	R	S	T	U
t	t	l	r	t	r	r
V	W	X	Y	Z		
t	l	l	l	r		

Alphabet edit involves reading the letters of the alphabet aloud as a class or small group while completing the accompanying action. **l** is a left arm raise, **r** is a right arm raise and **t** is both arms together. A further variation (and complication) is to accompany the arm raise with an opposite leg raise!

r

l

t

Alphabet edit connects left and right brain, helps hand eye co-ordination and will improve visual, auditory and kinesthetic ability.

Some ways to relax your class

The best way to relax your class is to be relaxed yourself. Be well prepared and on time. Calm beginnings and endings to lessons give positive messages and minimize stress.

In some schools, very few students know what relaxation is. Fight and flight, territoriality and other reptilian behaviours are, for some, the norm rather than the exception. Teaching and then regularly using relaxation techniques will surprise you with its benefits. Here are two methods.

Relaxing the parts

'Firstly close your eyes and then one stage at a time relax each part of your body. Breathe evenly and gently. As you progress, repeat to yourself in a progressively slower monotone:

now I relax my eyes
now I relax my mouth
now I relax my neck
now I relax my shoulders
now I relax my arms
now I relax my chest
now I relax my stomach
now I relax my legs
now I relax my feet'

Belly breathing

Sit or stand in an upright position. Place your clasped hands on your stomach. Breathe evenly and gently. Breathe from your belly first, filling up your stomach and chest like a balloon. Continue to breathe as your chest rises. Continue to breathe into your throat. Then gently exhale. Repeat the exercise. It may help to visualize the air filling up like a balloon as you go.

Using music

Selectively used, music can enhance the learning environment in a number of ways. It can be used as part of an active or passive concert, to energize or relax, set a theme or eliminate 'white noise'.

Brain Wave *Normal Activity*

BETA β
13–25 CPS

This is the brain wave of your 'concious' mind. It characterises logical thought, analysis and action. You are wide awake and alert, figuring out complex problems, talking, speaking, doing.

ALPHA α
8–12 CPS

This is the brain wave that characterizes relaxation and meditation. The state of mind during which you daydream and let your imagination run away. It is a state of relaxed alertness, facilitating inspiration, fast assimilation of facts and heightened memory. Alpha lets you reach your subconcious, and since your self-image is primarily in your sub-concious, it is the only effective way to reach it.

THETA θ
4–7 CPS

Deep mediation and reverie. The twilight zone associated with creativity, high suggestibility and flashes of inspiration. Dominant during ages 2-5.

DELTA δ
0.5–3 CPS

Deep dreamless sleep.

(Colin Rose, *Accelerated Learning)*

According to recent research the playing of Mozart co-ordinates breathing, cardiovascular rhythms and brain wave rhythm and acts on the unconscious, stimulating receptivity and perception. Baroque music – Bach, Pachelbel, Handel, Vivaldi – which has a beat of 60-70 beats per minute induces an Alpha state brain wave cycle: 60–70 beats per minute is about the rhythm of the resting heart. The Alpha state is one of relaxed alertness where receptivity to storing of new information is high.

In Dr Lozanov's language learning, Baroque music is used as an integral part of **passive or concert review**. This review occurs at the conclusion of a session and is used to engage the whole brain. By using sensory based suggestive language to summarize content while the learners attune their listening to the music, long-term recall of the information is dramatically improved. An effective concert review will begin with the reader inviting the learners to relax, make themselves comfortable and begin to listen to the music. As the reader continues to speak with the voice just below the music, the learners are kept in a relaxed state. The content is recalled in summary and the learners are invited to consider the applications and uses they can put the new knowledge to. To close the concert review, the reader gently brings the listeners back to the present as the music fades.

An **active concert** is a reading where the voice modulates according to the movement of the music: the voice rides the music lending it, and the content of the reading, dramatic emphasis. An active concert is a powerful way of inputting new information. It is used consistently as part of many Accelerated Learning language programmes.

Music can be used to energize or relax. By turning the volume down to a point where it is just perceptible when there is quiet in the room 'white noise' - the hum of lights, heating systems, and so on – can be overcome and a supportive calm ambience generated.

It is best to avoid the tribalism which often comes with playing students' own music. Once you have agreed protocols for the use of music and you are seen to use it as part of the learning you can perhaps begin to experiment. Generally it is best to use instrumental music, with music with lyrics confined to special breaks or energizers. Personal stereos are not a good idea in classrooms!

Some suggested choices for different purposes are outlined below. These are pieces which I have used or know have been used. The list is far from complete but may be a good starting point.

Establish a positive learning attitude
Create the atmosphere you seek by selective choice of music

- What a Wonderful World: Louis Armstrong
- Let's Work Together: Canned Heat
- Celebration: Kool and the Gang
- Stand By Me: Ben E King
- Oh What a Beautiful Morning: Rogers and Hammerstein
- Heal the World: Michael Jackson
- Simply the Best: Tina Turner

Provide a break state or demarcate time on task or for fun!

- Theme from *Jaws*
- Epic Movie Soundtracks (*Chariots of Fire, Close Encounters, Star Wars,* and so on)
- *Flintstones, Twilight Zone, Mission Impossible* and other TV theme tunes

Energize or relax

- Hallelujah Chorus: Handel
- William Tell Overture: Rossini
- New World Symphony: Dvorak
- Trois Gymnopedies: Satie
- Prélude a l'après-midi d'un faune Debussy

Focus concentration and enhance imagination

- Violin Concerto nos 1 and 3: Mendelssohn
- Optima learning nos 1 and 2: Barzakov
- Relax with the Classics: LIND Institute
- Watermark: Enya

Used as a revision tool or as part of a learning journey

- Tubular Bells: Mike Oldfield
- The Four Seasons: Vivaldi
- Masterpieces: Sky
- Earth Tribe Rhythms: Lewis
- A Week in the Real World: Womad and Peter Gabriel

As part of a multisensory learning experience

- Oxygene: Jean Michel Jarre
- Various: Gypsy Kings
- Friends on the Road: Bundhu Boys
- Welela: Miriam Makeba
- Folon: Salif Keita

Active concert

– Piano Concerto no 5:	Beethoven
– Symphony nos 93 and 94:	Haydn
– Violin Concerto nos 4 and 5:	Mozart

Provide inspiration and motivation

– Chariots of Fire:	Vangelis
– Fanfare for the Common Man:	Copeland
– We Will Rock You:	Queen
– Thus Spake Zarathustra	Strauss

Accentuate theme oriented units

- Native people's selections: for example, Australian Aborigine, American Indian, Inca
- Recordings on environmental themes by Steven Halpern, Kitaro Big Band, Trad Jazz, Marching Bands
- Celtic folk and Celtic rock

Concert review

– Brandenburg Concertos nos 2 and 5:	Bach
– Canon in D:	Pachelbel
– Music for the Royal fireworks:	Handel
– Four Seasons:	Vivaldi

Memory Map of the learning environment

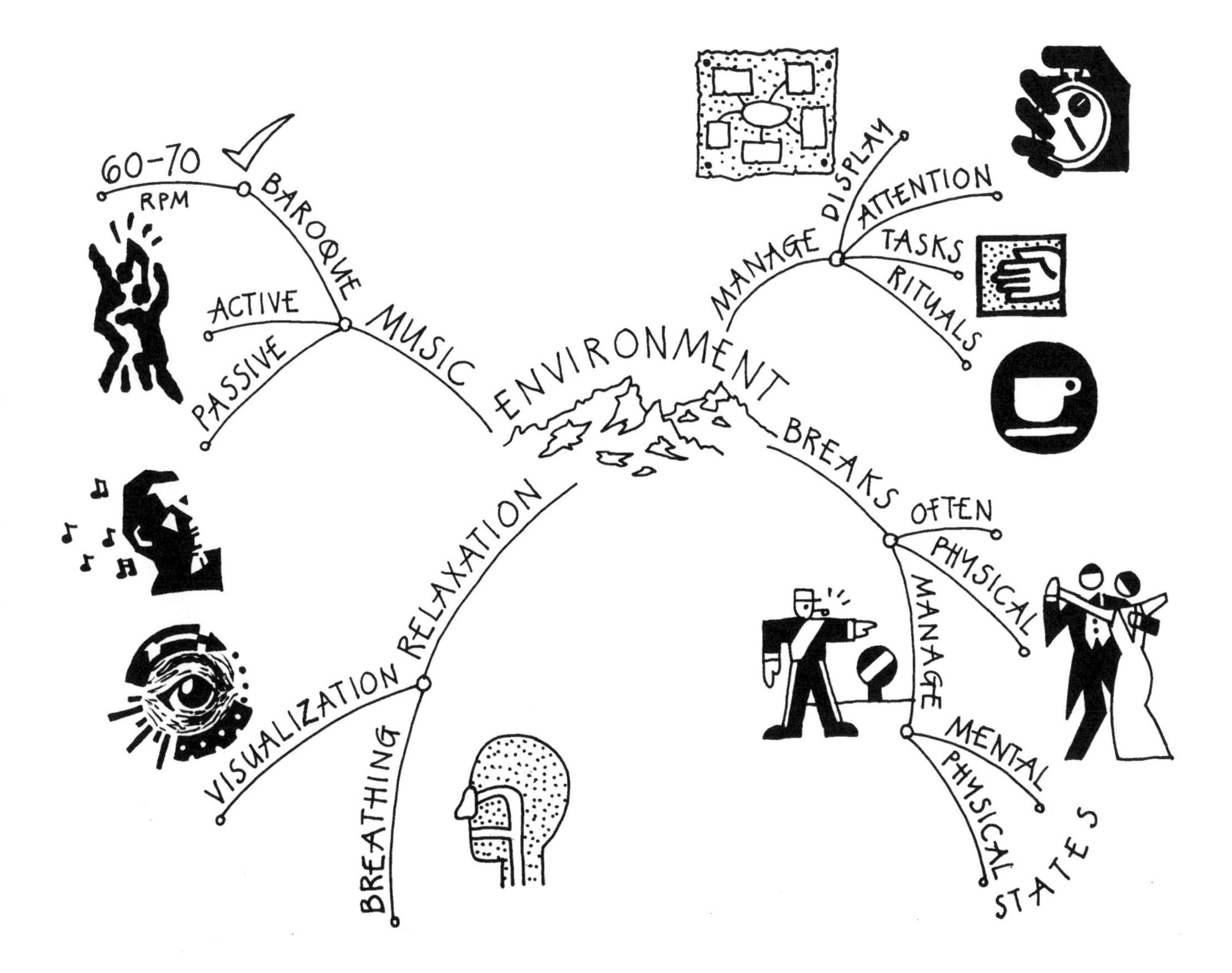

Review

Key questions about the learning environment

- what specific teaching rituals can you use to improve your lessons?
- in what ways can learning be said to take place unconsciously?
- why is individualized learning important?
- when and how might Brain Gym® activities help your students?
- what techniques might relax the learners in your class?
- how might Baroque music help long-term learning?
- what are the key points about language during a concert review?

Accessing and retaining information

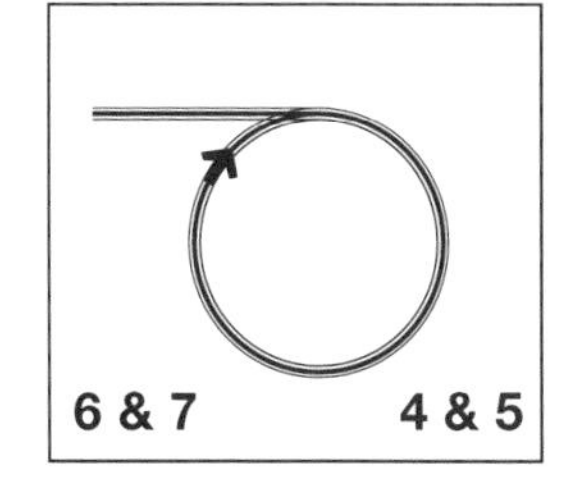

In Section Five you will learn how ...

- ***we can best access and retain information***
- ***the SCOTS CLAN MAPS model summarizes all the key ways to remember learning points***
- ***skim and speed reading techniques can be taught***
- ***memory mapping utilizes both the left and right brain***
- ***to use preview and review techniques to improve recall by as much as 90 per cent***
- ***recall in learning drops by as much as 80 per cent within 24 hours***
- ***to develop time and priority management skills***

Accessing and retaining the information

In order to access the information that a student needs, he or she will need to know the answer to the key question, 'What do I need this information for?' Encourage students to list some summary responses to this question before they begin to read a text, watch a video, listen to a lecture or begin a project. A refinement could be a description of the application of the new skills or knowledge in VAK. 'As a result of reading this book I see myself .... I hear myself saying ... and I feel ....'

Using the video shop method described later in this section, learners should get the Big Picture first. This may mean flicking though a book first or asking for a summary from a lecturer or teacher before input or reading the programme notes of a video or radio recording.

Eating the elephant. How does one eat an elephant? (Let's assume one wants to!) The answer is one piece at a time! Similarly with a large and seemingly overwhelming learning task. Break it down into small units and provide incentives for consuming each piece. This process is also described in detail later in this section. The learner should begin to break the content of a text down into more manageable units. Referring back to the original key questions prioritize the order in which you begin to consume each smaller piece. Allocate time spent on each on a similar basis.

By identifying prompt questions and having them to hand as the text is read, the learner is taxed to think around and through the issues. Prompts which produce clarification, application and summary are useful.

Key

Applications

Personal

Evidence

Deduced

Some suggested prompts are:

- What are the **K**ey points in summary?
- Are there any **A**pplications for this new information?
- Are there **P**ersonal uses for the new information?
- What is the **E**vidence for the truth of this information ?
- What can be **D**educed from the new information?

Students should use the study methods which work best for them. An understanding of their preferred learning style, which representation system they operate naturally in and an awareness of their balance of intelligences will legitimize their choices of methods. However, this is a sophistication which may be beyond their developmental stage or their experience. By using other students to model effective study patterns young learners can quickly get an appreciation that there are many different yet equally effective ways of accessing information. Modelling involves detailed questioning of what steps are taken when a learner successfully engages with and learns new and challenging material. Students can work in small groups interviewing one person who is particularly strong in an area of academic work. The same questions are asked, the answers noted and then compared.

Questions which could be asked include:

- What is a subject that you can learn easily?
- Which topic in that subject are you most pleased with learning easily?
- When you were learning that topic, what were your aims/goals/objectives?
- How did you know you were learning successfully?
- What were you seeing? Hearing? Feeling?
- When you set out to learn something new what are the first things you do?
- When you are learning something new do you see it in pictures? or hear words? or is it a feeling?
- If you see it in pictures, what are they like? Are they bright? Big? Colourful?
- If you hear it, whose voice do you hear? Who is speaking to whom? What sort of voice is it?
- If it's a feeling, what sort of feeling is it?
- How do you remember the new information? In pictures? Words? Feelings?
- When you find the information difficult, what do you do? What makes it easier?
- When you need the information for a test or an exam how do you recall it?

Modelling helps displace the myth that successful learners happen to be 'cleverest'. It may be that they are simply more methodical, better organized, have discovered their preferred learning styles or are processing the information in their preferred intelligences.

By utilizing tools and techniques learners can save time and enagage with the material more easily. These techniques are in themselves very simple but students are seldom taught them.

Teach your students to try the following techniques:

Index cards
Keywords can be written on index cards to summarize a topic or stage in a process. On the other side a coloured visual or symbol of some sort can be used to help recall. Turn them over and attempt to summarize the content. By mixing them up and then sequencing them, stages in processes can be learned.

Post-its
Stick post-its with key vocabulary written on them around the study, bedroom and hallway. Again, they can be ordered and re-ordered on a flat surface. Good for preparing essays!

Posters
Dramatic and colourful posters which visually summarize important content can be placed at eye level or above.

Review to music
An enjoyable, easy way to memorize essential summary information. Music with 60–70 beats per minute is especially good for inducing an Alpha brain wave state – for long-term memory.

Dramatic monologue
Parts of the text or the summarized key points spoken aloud can help with recall, particularly if the voices are outrageous!

Get a manager
An arrangement whereby someone other than the teacher agrees to listen to, test or interrogate the learner at a pre-agreed time.

Walkabout
Make recall distinctive by memorizing new information in an unusual location. Different chapters in a book can be learned in different rooms. Put index cards on the floor in sequence and walk between each, memorizing as you go. This helps kinesthetic recall.

Raps, rhythm or rhyme
Put something in verse or to music and make it rhyme and it becomes easier to remember. Accompany it by a suitable movement or gesture. Good for dates, kings and queens, mathematical tables and formulae, periodic tables, lists of facts.

Visualization
Place the information into your visual memory by making it bright, colourful, moving, attached to a person, place or object and big. To remember difficult spellings, visualize the word in bright, bold and colourful units chunked together. Store them as a picture in the upper visual field. You should be able to 'see' it there when you need to.

Ridiculous applications
The unusual and outrageous are immediately memorable. By taking the information out of context and giving it ridiculous applications it 'sticks'. Try imagining the Queen and the Pope hitting each other with feather pillows in a boxing ring while shouting out differing views about the Reformation!

Highlighter pens
Highlighter pens can be used to highlight key words so that they stick out on subsequent readings. In languages, use different colours for different parts of the sentence.

Memory maps
Described in detail later in this section, memory maps can be displayed, shared, added to, built up and cut up. They are non-hierarchical and connect left and right brain through their use of strong visuals, patterning and keywords.

Faces and places
A memory technique which relies on attaching or tagging some information to a place or face the learner knows really well. In recalling the face or place, the information accompanies it. A similar technique is to take the information and break it down into basic elements and then build up a story around each of these elements connecting them in as colourful, humorous and outrageous a way as possible.

Build maps
Old wallpaper, the backs of posters and discarded Christmas paper can be scavenged and put into use as a summary map of a whole syllabus for a student to pin to his or her bedroom wall. Any combination of memory mapping, flow-charting, keywording and highlighting which is bright and visible will be effective.

Insist lists
Lists of essential information placed on pocket-handy card and kept with you at all times.

The final stages are: Show You Know and Review it or Lose it. Review is dealt with in detail later in this section. Show You Know involves the teacher and learner finding opportunities to demonstrate their new knowledge and understanding, either for their own satisfaction to agreed standards or to someone else.

Recall and Memory: the SCOTS CLAN MAPS memory model

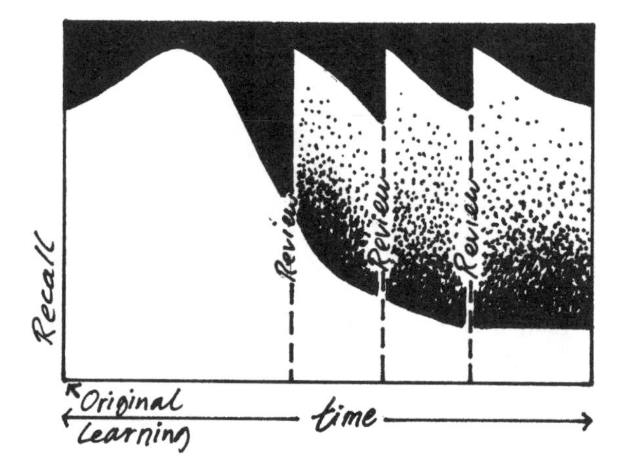

Without immediate, then regular, review of new information, recall can drop by as much as 80 per cent within 24 hours.

The diagram shows the impact of review upon recall. The importance of regular and distinctive review cannot be over-emphasized.

Recall in the long-term memory requires an experience to have significance to the brain and its storage systems. We generally remember items which are demarcated by being of significance to our reticular system. Data of value is more likely to be filtered in, data deemed of less significance is filtered out. To make data more significant, attach it to a positive emotion, desire or need. Hence the significance of positive learner goals. To further add to the chances of storage in the long-term memory, make the data distinctive by attaching it to a sensory experience (sight; sound; feeling; taste; smell). Experiences which are unique; absurd; vivid; colourful; sexual; or powerfully emotional are more easily remembered, associating an experience through any of these makes it instantly more memorable. Classifying experiences, sequencing them, linking them to a numerical or linguistic pattern or locating them with a well-known place, person, time or event will also help impact on the long-term memory.

These are the underlying practices of what have become known as memory improvement techniques. To help you remember them, think of a remote highland glen. You've gone to visit Alistair of McCalistair but have got lost. As the highland cattle sniff nosily around your kilt you remember that in your sporran you have a copy of ...

The SCOTS CLAN MAPS memory model

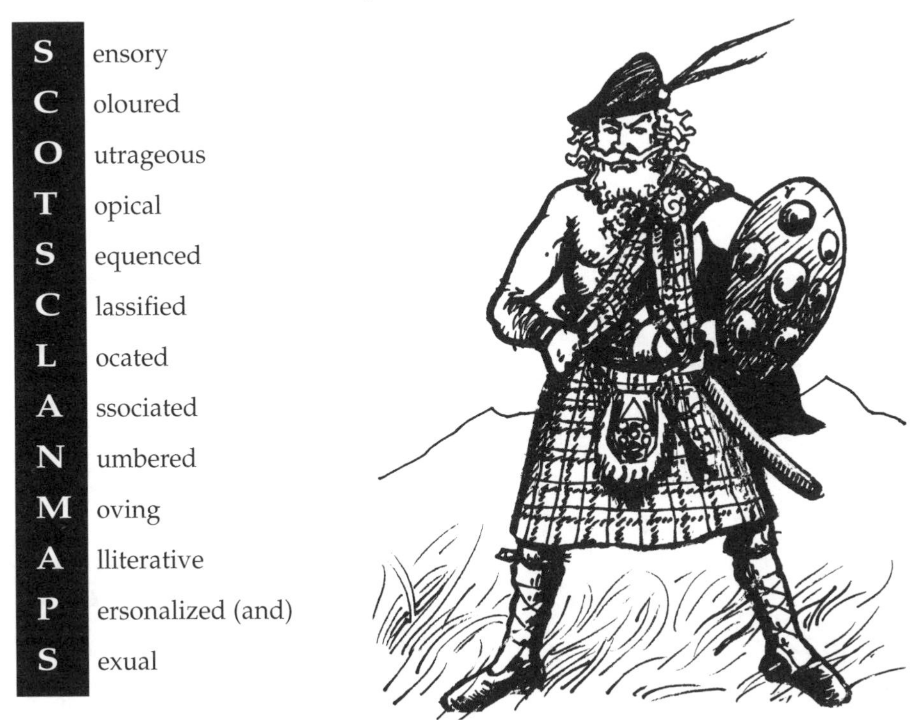

A good example of applying the SCOTS CLAN MAPS is to utilize it to recall lists of words or items in sequence, or names and dates. The planets in the solar system in increasing distance from the Sun are: Mercury, Venus, Earth, Mars, Jupiter, Saturn, Uranus, Neptune, Pluto. A way of remembering them might be to visualize a moving sequence of related images which is colourful, outrageous and topical. The images can be linked together in story form. For example:

> Freddie Mercury is with a beautiful woman called Venus and into the earth around them they are placing Mars bars. Into the picture comes a Jew called Peter who brings with him an urn. He is sat on the urn. Freddie Mercury and Venus ask him, 'Why don't you run us?' To start the race, Neptune raises his trident. Pluto presents the prizes.

The more specific the images are to the learner, the easier they will be to remember. Any memory strategy which can attach the content to something which is known, while at the same time making each element special to the learner, will have a chance of success. The story sequence can be easily learned. It belongs to the learner. A mnemonic is similar. Richard of York gave battle in vain, describes the colours of the spectrum. A tag system works in the same way. The learner takes a place which is well known. Let's say it's the street where he or she lives. The learner knows all the houses and all the occupants, the house numbers, the colours of each door and the layout of gardens. To learn the historical events in the period from 1789, each house in the street can take on the associations of a particular event or significant moment. As we move up the street, so we progress through history.

At number 27, Mrs Smith's, there's a revolution taking place. In the front garden they've set up a guillotine and they're chopping the heads off the flowers. Louis XVI and Marie Antoinette are sitting outside eating cakes. On the side of Mrs Smith's house, a sign says, 'To the Bastille'. Her three little children aged 7, 8 and 9 are selling tickets for the show. Mrs Smith is shouting out the names of the characters at the top of her voice!

It is possible to build up an imaginary sequential visualization of historical events by tagging the detail to well-known places, making the action bright and colourful, dressing up the neighbours as historical figures and attaching key dates to each front door.

Utilize the SCOTS CLAN MAPS model to make any content easier to remember.

Skim and speed reading

Like other forms of language comprehension, reading connects symbols to trigger reference experiences. The more pleasant the trigger reference experiences, the more you want to read and the more easy it becomes. The more easy, the more likely that you will comprehend and retain the material. Reading does not require sub-vocalization for comprehension. You don't have to say it or hear it in your head to understand it. Because we learn spoken language first we tend towards an auditory strategy for reading. This poses a difficulty because there is an underlying belief that there is only meaning when a word is 'said'. The need to say words slows up the reading process. Meaning can be gleaned from the visual appearance of a word or sequence of words without sub-vocalization and so reading can be quicker and smoother. You can look at a crowd of people and see several people at once and you can look at a whole sentence or paragraph and see several words at once.

There is an optimal physiology which accompanies effective speed reading. It is that which is unique to you and which comes when you are in eager anticipation of an achievement which is certain. When you are relaxed but alert and when you are physically comfortable. Unconscious associations about reading being difficult and taxing, open our inability to move through the material very quickly. Removing these associations is the first step. You should then place the text so that it is in the upper field of your vision and so that with your peripheral vision you can take in the whole page. Before beginning, do you know what you want to read for? Have you given yourself the Big Picture? How does this connect with what went before and what's to come?

Next visualize two things. The first is what you already know. See it as a moving or still image. Then an image of the text's central theme. Place your image of the central theme in your 'mind's eye' to be surrounded by the new related themes. Place your tongue between your teeth if you want to avoid sub-vocalizing! Scan your eyes down the page. Look for keywords. The 'of's'and 'it's' are not necessary for your comprehension. Move more quickly than you are comfortable with and use a scanning pattern which suits you.

To help students with speed and skim reading the video shop model helps. Speed and skim-reading skills are similar to those used when visiting a supermarket or a video shop. You begin by selecting the best store for your needs. In doing so you already have a sense of its value to you and what you hope to come away with. You know where it is and its approximate size and have some confidence in discovering quickly where all the contents are to be found. Once there you find what you want by getting the overview first, moving quickly to the sections you need and only then looking at the products in any detail. In the video shop you get a sense of the content of each video from location of the shelf, the relationship to the other videos placed around it and by the images, words and pictures placed together on the box. No one reads every word on every video box in the shop! You can understand without needing to!

So, to speed read a book follow the video shop principle ...

- Scan the reading material quickly to get a feel for its layout and organization. Flick through the pages. Find the index and look at the items there. For each chapter or section described in the contents page, skim through assessing its length and organization.
- Relax and make yourself comfortable. Be clear about what you need from the text.
- Take some summary notes or memory map what you already know about the topic you are going to read about; build these up as you go along. Visualize the central theme and place it in the centre of your mind's eye.
- read for understanding by looking for key paragraphs, sentences and words.
- use a pen, pencil or finger to help you speed down either:
  a paragraph at a time
  the centre of the page
  a slalom down the page
- to help you avoid reading every word, place your tongue between your teeth and concentrate on taking in all the information! Move back up and down the page if you feel you need to.
- stay in relaxed alertness by taking regular breaks; changing position; walking around.

The memory mapping technique
A memory map is a flexible revision and summary tool which utilises left and right brain, orders ad hoc thoughts, can be built up and added to, highlights links and is bold, vivid and colourful. A memory map activates the patterning capacity of the brain. The main topic is placed in the centre of the map and subsidiary ideas radiate out from the centre with further related points radiating from them. Each main topic and subsidiary idea should have a bold and distinctive visual image attached to it. The images should represent the author's understanding of the topic. Memory maps should include connecting lines, arrows and rows of dots to link related topics in ways which are unique to the author.

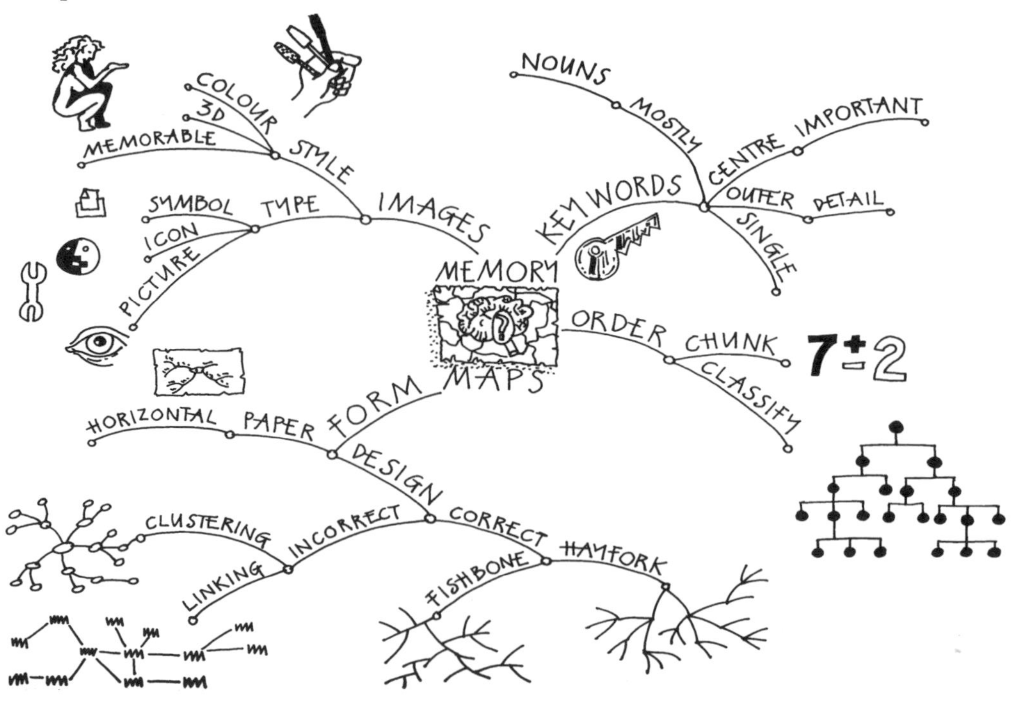

Review and recall in learning

Different review techniques are available to the classroom teacher to be used before, during or after lessons. Students should be encouraged to learn and use the techniques independently.

Self-questioning

As students work on new material they should be asking themselves questions like:
'How well do I understand this topic?'
'How might I explain or teach it to someone else? What are the key points?'
'How would someone else know I had learned and understood it?'
'What are the applications of the new knowledge?'

Instant feedback

The teacher uses a traffic light system with red for not yet understood, amber for understood and green for fully understood and checks it out with the class. Another way is for a show of hands, 'On a scale of one to five, show me how well you are understanding this topic?' Students hold up hands with a number of fingers.

Chained review

Assign a chunk of an extended topic to an individual, pair or group and then ask each in turn to present back to the others, so that once completed, the whole topic has been reviewed.

Written prompt questions

As described earlier in this section, prompt questions such as the KAPED – key points, applications, personal uses, evidence of truth, deductions – can be used to act as a checklist.

Paired review

'In pairs describe three key things/the most important points/the most useful information you have learned. Agree one question you'd like an answer to.'

Memory map review

'Individually construct a memory map of the topic, then share it with a partner and explain its construction.'

Individual, pairs and fours

Time is set aside for individual reflection on the learning, it is then shared in pairs with a focusing question such as: 'Agree and prioritize the most important information needed for an exam.'

Active listening

Individuals are assigned an active learning role prior to the teachers giving an input or listening to a guest speaker or watching a video and the individual adopts that role. The same roles are spread around the class. Those with the same role meet and agree their findings before re-organizing into different groups. Thus each re-organized group has a number of individuals within it who have been listening for different purposes. Example roles for an older group are:

- Summarizes – succinctly summarizes the new information
- Questions – asks questions in order to clarify
- Applies – provides examples of practical application
- Relates – finds supportive examples from own experience
- Disagrees – opens up further discussion on areas of disagreement
- Prioritizes – puts key points in order of importance

By operating this way, group discussion is structured and everyone contributes at some point.

Collage
A collage of keywords, pictures, symbols, cuttings, quotes is produced.

Review against goals and/or objectives
The teacher sets the lesson objectives out at the beginning of the lesson and reviews them at the end. Similarly if the individual learner has set out objectives they can be reviewed.

Each one – teach one
In pairs one student has the responsibility of 'teaching' the content to another. Then they swap.

Quizzes – crosswords – anagrams – wordsearches
Either set by the teacher or by students.

Rap or rhyme or mime
The key content is summarized in one of these forms.

Presentation
Individuals, pairs or groups make a presentation to an audience of peers or younger students or an invited audience.

Concert review
A summarized review of content, read to music with a beat of 60–70 beats per minute. Baroque music is good for this.

Koosh ball
In a circle or circles each student describes a key idea or word or concept when he or she has the ball. Best done in smaller groups with time spent beforehand on what could be included.

Outrageous applications
Encourage descriptions of the most absurd applications of new information. A fun game is to link left and right brain in a relaxed atmosphere.

Journey around the room
Using peripherals, flashbacks and flashcards. Topics can be outlined on visual displays, either stuck up at eye level or above around the room or on different cards. Students then go to each in turn, talking through what is described there and how it all ties together.

Time and priority management for learners

Planning

People

Personality

There are three sources of pressure on a learner's time. They are the three **P**s. The ability to **p**lan ahead, the ability to manage other **p**eople and their expectations, and the **p**ersonality of the learner. Each source of pressure can vary over time, as does the ability to deal with it.

Planning is about making deliberate choices about what to do and when.

People is about dealing effectively with those around you.

Personality is about how tasks and issues are approached.

Managing planning

Clarity about personal goals, targets and tasks helps in planning ahead. Students with well-specified personal goals will be more likely to be successful in their time and priority management. When, as a result of a goal-setting activity or a counselling interview or a succession of academic homeworks, tasks begin to emerge which conflict with other loyalties, it will be easier for the student who has clear personal goals to make judgements about priorities. In the absence of such reference points prioritizing becomes more difficult.

Priority lists

Students ought to be encouraged to identify all the tasks they are required to complete both in their personal and home lives and in their academic work. These tasks can then be broken down into short, medium and long term: perhaps today, this week, this month, this term. Once a sense of time constraints emerges the tasks can be further prioritized using the **ABC method**. **A** tasks must be done. **B** tasks ought to be done. **C** tasks could be done. It might look something like this:

Today		This week		This month		This term
Spar interview form	A	complete Spar form	B	attend band practice	A	catch up on coursework
letter to Gran	C	visit Charlie in hospital	C	complete coursework	A	work to revision timetable
new trainers	C	Friday talk preparation	A	time at leisure centre	C	write up GNVQ placement
check maths homework	A	GNVQ talk	A	begin revision timetable	B	residential visit
meet Chris for coffee	C	arrange next placement	B	put money in bank	A	band performances
phone Toni	B	tickets for annual ball	B	sort out part-time job	B	annual ball
band practice (4.00)	A	pay back £10 to Dad	C	re-organize notes	C	careers interview
clean bedroom	C	return library CDs	A	meet T for study sessions	B	college applications
prepare GNVQ talk	B	party Sat – pressie?	B	cash expenses cheque	A	portfolio for interviews
buy new pen	B	maths formulae learned	A	pay for residential course	B	London trip
reading for Friday group	B	arrange loan of camera	C	GNVQ placement	A	
		English reading list from AS	A	English essays on novel	B	
		homework club	B	Spar interview form	A	

The time management system is based on the To Do list. A To Do list is written, prioritised and revised daily. Planning cycles should start with long-term tasks first. For students this could mean identifying all the prioritized tasks for the term and writing them down. Then out of these will fall monthly tasks and others. Then there will be weekly tasks then daily To Do lists. In prioritizing they should use the **ABC method** and apply the **Pareto principle**. Ask them to identify which 20 per cent of tasks will give them the maximum benefit? Which 20 per cent will best help them achieve the goals they seek. These ought to be **A** tasks and begun immediately. A good time manager deals with tasks as they become important, not when they are already urgent.

For **A** tasks they need to schedule quality time in which to complete them. This may mean blocking out certain times of the late afternoon, evening or weekend, for work. Students should get themselves into this discipline of scheduling time for themselves and building rituals around it. For example, their **A** time may be for an hour and a half between 6.00 and 7.30, four evenings a week. During this time they contract with themselves, family and friends that they will not be disturbed, interrupted with phone calls, asked to wash dishes or expected to walk the dog. A set of expectations are built around this ritual. The student commits to spend the time in an environment which encourages the study outcomes they seek. This may be a bedroom, a library, a table in the kitchen or anywhere else which can be an effective and positive 'anchor' for study.

Ideally the **A** time will occur when the learner's energy levels are up. There should also be the opportunity for regular mini-breaks with little incentive rewards built in.

Managing other people

Avoid interruptions by firstly being aware of what and who causes them. Students who seek interruptions study in social areas and areas where there are things to be seen, listened to or talked about with others. Students who avoid interruptions are consistent in their study regime and the rituals surrounding it. They take themselves away from unhelpful distractions. They also learn how to say no when they feel they need to!

Simple assertiveness techniques such as the five part 'I' message, the broken record technique, asking for time or softening the content help the student to say no when a major disruption threatens.

The five part 'I' message involves:

- Stage one: **objective description of the other person's behaviour**
  'This is the third time you've asked me to go out tonight.'
- Stage two: **the result of that behaviour**
  'When you keep interrupting I lose my train of thought.'
- Stage three: **feelings about that behaviour**
  'It makes me feel as though you are not really interested in what I'm doing and it annoys me.'
- Stage four: **request for a change**
  'I can't come and I'd like you to stop interrupting me.'
- Stage five: **invitation to reply**
  'How do you feel about that?'

With the 'broken record' technique you are trying to be very clear about what you want without getting angry, uncomfortable, irritated or loud. Identify what you want and make a clear statement – 'I can't go out this evening.' Repeat it without picking up any other counter statements so that you sound like a broken record – 'I can't go out this evening. I'm sorry, I can't go out this evening.'

Asking for time helps you assess your priorities. You simply ask for time to think over what's being asked of you. You specify the time you need to think over the pros and cons and tell the other person you will get back to them.

- ☛ listen to the request
- ☛ clarify and make sure you understand what's being asked of you
- ☛ pause, take a breath and think about it
- ☛ acknowledge the request of the other person and say that you have understood it
- ☛ say, 'I can't decide now, I need time to think about it.'
- ☛ tell the other person how much time you need and how and when you will get back to them

Softening content involves five stages too. It is a way of taking the anger out of a situation and getting the compromise you want.

- Stage one: **an explanation**
  'I can't go out tonight as I've got some work to finish.'
- Stage two: **recognition of the other person's position**
  'I know you're disappointed.'
- Stage three: **a positive stroke**
  'It's really nice of you to ask.'
- Stage four: **an apology**
  'I feel really bad about it.'
- Stage five: **a mutually acceptable compromise**
  'How about tomorrow?'

Managing yourself
Students can usefully use the techniques on goal-setting and anchoring to get themselves in the right frame of mind for study. However, we are all very cunning at avoiding starting and have developed sophisticated procrastination skills! Procrastination is something we all do. It can sometimes be positive. Sometimes a slight delay in acting allows a more considered decision to be taken; it can encourage creativity, and it allows scope for consultation. It is important to develop the self-understanding to be able to identify when it happens and why. We all put off unpleasant tasks, particularly if they involve people and confrontation.

Our patterns of procrastination follow our own personality traits. You may recognize yourself from one or more of these:

The **Self-Doubter** consistently believes that they are not good enough and not quite up to successfully achieving the task.
The **Perfectionist** is never happy with the outcome and wants to refine it or its planning down to the last detail.
The **Rebel** chooses to see the task as a threat to their identity. They avoid doing the task as a way of asserting their identity.
The **Excessive-Socializer** finds endless ways of avoiding doing the task. They find people to discuss their procrastination with and seemingly cannot find the time to make a beginning.
The **Daydreamer** cannot get onto or stay on task. Their mind wanders off onto other topics because the task seems so overwhelming.

The **Priority-Invertor** does all the other insignificant things to avoid the **A** tasks. Their consolation is in always appearing busy.

Procrastination invariably causes stress. Tasks nag at us to be done. Our self-justification at not doing them can get increasingly absurd. Sometimes the stress arises because of poor time management or prioritizing. It may be that you have allowed yourself to accept a task with ill-defined instructions or with insufficient time or without knowing the standard required. The outcome is that tasks can appear overwhelming.

With seemingly overwhelming tasks you complete them by breaking them down into elements and doing each related task one at a time (eat the elephant one bite at a time). The list below helps break tasks into bite-size, achievable chunks. By working through it, a student can overcome the fear of beginning.

1. Deal directly with the delay
    a. What is it I'm afraid of?
    b. What's the worst thing that can happen?
    c. How might I prevent it?

2. Establish the real cost of delay
    a. What are the consequences of my delaying?
    b. How does my delaying affect others?

3. Stress the benefits
    a. What plusses start when this is done?
    b. What minuses stop?

4. Reward yourself
    a. How will I reward myself along the way and on completion?

5. Seek support
    a. How can I involve others and make the task easier?

Memory Map of accessing and retaining information

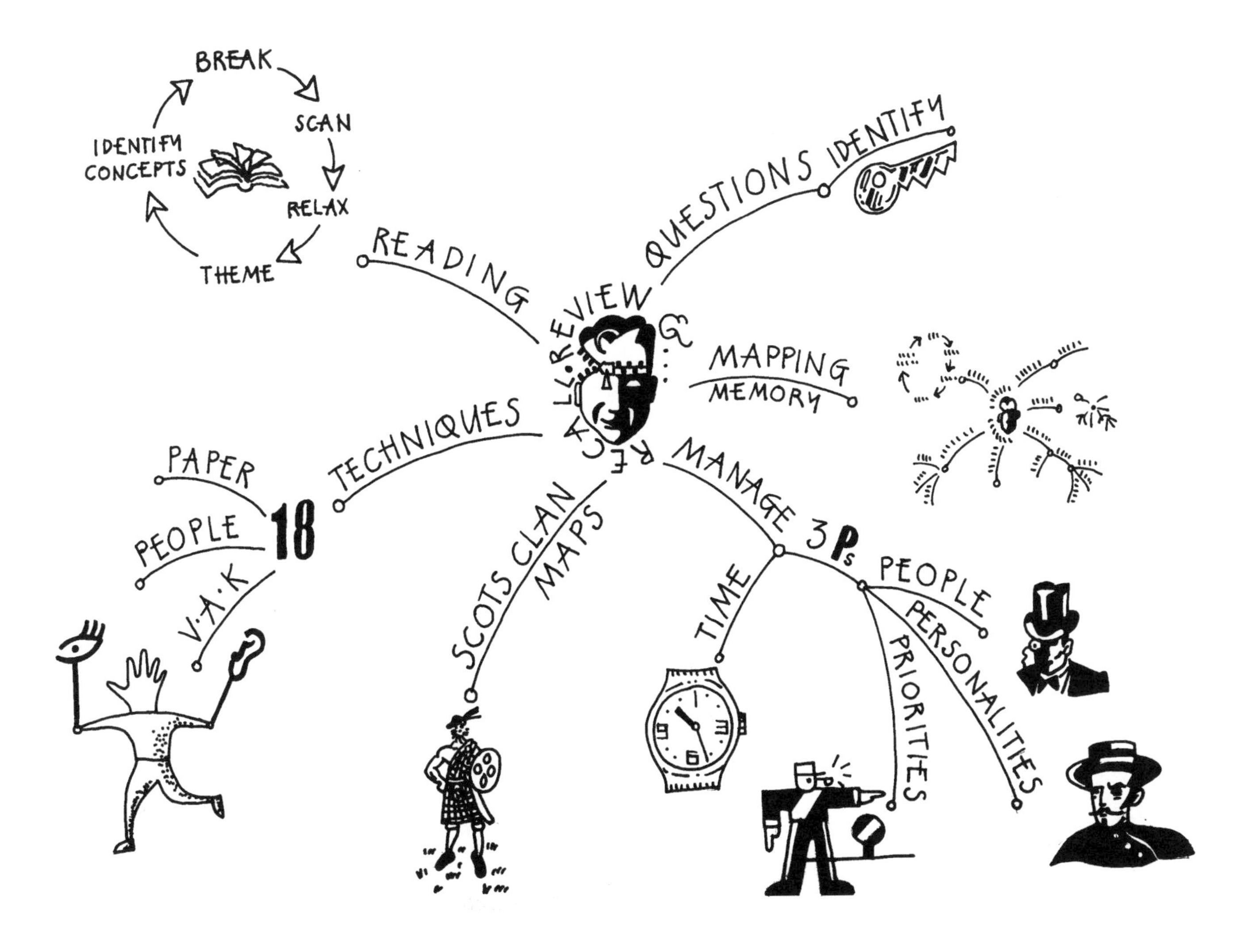

Review

Key questions about accessing and retaining information ...

- what steps can your students take to improve their ability to get the information they need?
- how does review impact on recall?
- in what ways do we best remember information?
- what is the significance of the SCOTS CLAN MAPS memory model to learners in your class?
- which review techniques will work best for your classes?
- why is the skim and speed-reading technique like visiting the video shop?
- what actions should students take to improve their time and priority management?

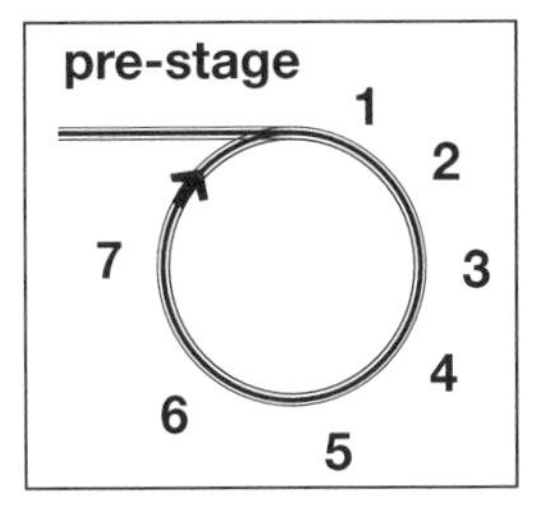

Twenty-one ways to improve learning

In this section, 21 of the key points are assembled as a checklist and summary.

1. ***Build on the BASIS model constantly***

The self-esteem and self-belief of the learner underlies all learning. Build in reward and reinforcement systems at school, department and class levels. Practise them within lessons.

2. ***Use relaxation or energizing techniques to access a state of relaxed alertness***

By using relaxation exercises or Brain Gym®, you can help the learners become more resourceful for learning. These tools will help alleviate induced learner anxiety.

3. ***Be congruent in setting high expectations***

Apply your messages consistently. Your expectations as a teacher will be passed on consciously and unconsciously.

4. ***Use positive, affirming language***

Be specific in describing the behaviours you want. Be choosy about your choice of language. When you say 'don't' it will carry an embedded message to do! 'Don't look down!' results in the person looking down immediately! Reinforce the positive messages by a positive, unconditional, stroking regime.

5. ***Pre-process***

Advise learners beforehand of topics or issues which will be covered. Use visual displays of how the work for the year maps out. Make reference to the different points on the map as the year progresses. Build a sense of a journey with an ultimate destination and different milestones along the way. Encourage some advance thinking on, or related to, each topic or issue as they come up. Use opening activities like, 'Write down all you know about....' Have learners work in pairs or small groups to collect all they know about a topic before formal teaching about that topic.

6. *Give the Big Picture first (the advanced organizer)*

For each session describe, or have the students describe, the learning that will take place and the learning outcomes. Use a section of your chalkboard or similar to outline the learning outcomes starting with, 'By the end of this session you will...'

Encourage learners to link the session outcomes to their own learning goals.

7. *Chunk it down*

Start from the whole topic and break it down. The most items or chunks of information an individual readily and immediately remembers is seven. Seven plus or minus two is often quoted as the optimum. Remember that right-brain learners need to start from the whole before any sequencing.

8. *Connect left and right for whole brain learning and input through VAK*

Monitor the type of experiences the learners in your classroom have. Are they predominantly left- or right-brain experiences? Can you introduce new material in ways which will access left and right? When inputting new material, utilize the main representational systems. For example, the brain in learning can be introduced by a short, summary talk; visual images and diagrams; replica brains; members of the class participating in a body sculpture to model the different functions; and discussion on the relevance of the new information. Limit the on-task time to no more than two minutes in excess of the students' chronological age, then change the task or review or utilize a break-state.

9. *Utilize the seven intelligences*

If we each learn in a preferred way then participation in a narrow range of learning experiences will disadvantage us. Firstly, establish what each learner's balance of intelligences is, by using the multiple intelligences questionnaire and then recording the results on the wheel. Then work across all seven intelligences as often as possible.

10. *Provide work at individual, pair and group level*

Structured peer learning with built-in safe opportunities for sharing understanding is a powerful aid to long-term learning.

11. *Use peripherals and archetypes*

Visual display of the subject material around the classroom improves the long-term learning by 90 per cent. Archetypes are positive role models. Individuals who have achieved in their field provide examples of positive learner behaviours.

12. ***Provide multi-path learning opportunities***

When possible, differentiate material by providing open-ended, problem-solving activities with a holistic approach to a topic. An informed application of differentiation in classrooms is one of the best starting points for Accelerated Learning.

13. ***Use spiral learning***

Introduce a complex topic by pre-processing, returning to it giving more time and attention and gradually build up work on that topic. This allows the unconscious mind to be processing the new information: sorting, selecting and connecting. On arriving at the topic in depth, the learner is more receptive to its complexities.

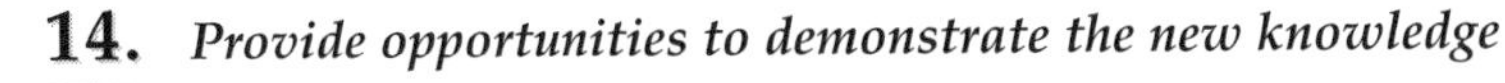

14. ***Provide opportunities to demonstrate the new knowledge***

Different opportunities in an environment which is safe for students to 'show they know'.

15. ***Build in review***

Eighty per cent of new knowledge is lost within 24 hours without some sort of review. Review the content of lessons at the end of each, and before beginning a new topic. Encourage review homeworks using memory maps or other activities across the seven intelligences.

16. ***Memory maps for note-taking***

Memory maps, when properly constructed, model the non-sequential, non-linear patterning capacity of the brain. By using colour, bold images and space on the page, learners build up their own unique way of making sense of the material.

17. ***Access the unconscious mind to help retain the new knowledge***

Careful choice of positive and specific language which reinforces successful and resourceful patterns of behaviour, alongside high expectations, is vital. You can use the 60–70 beats per minute of Baroque or similar music to induce the state of relaxed alertness which comes with the Alpha brain wave state. This will allow you to review large chunks of content and engage the conscious and unconscious mind simultaneously. You can also access the unconscious mind by using metaphor. Metaphor works by accessing the unconscious. The mind seeks to resolve open-ended questions. A metaphor introduced via a story is a powerful way of reinforcing learning, consciously and unconsciously.

18. *Teach time and priority management skills*

Help your students by teaching them the techniques described in this book and by regularly reviewing how they are coping. Encourage the exchange of good ideas and model successful time and priority managers.

19. *Anchor positive resource states*

Keep students feeling resourceful about what they are capable of achieving, by using the anchoring technique and being congruent in your expressions of support.

20. *Use creative visualizations*

Visualizations can work in a number of ways. By helping the learner access a previous past success through VAK, you can provide a tool for helping to reinforce a positive self-belief. It can also help some learners to develop an understanding of a complex topic by visualizing its different components.

21. *Build in fun!*

The time in our lives when we have had to learn most was at an early age when we explored, experimented, failed and tried again. If we can build in that open-mindedness, receptivity and sense of exploration to learning, then outcomes will be achieved more quickly, This is the basis on which Georgi Lozanov designed his Accelerated Learning language training with such startling results.

What to do next ...

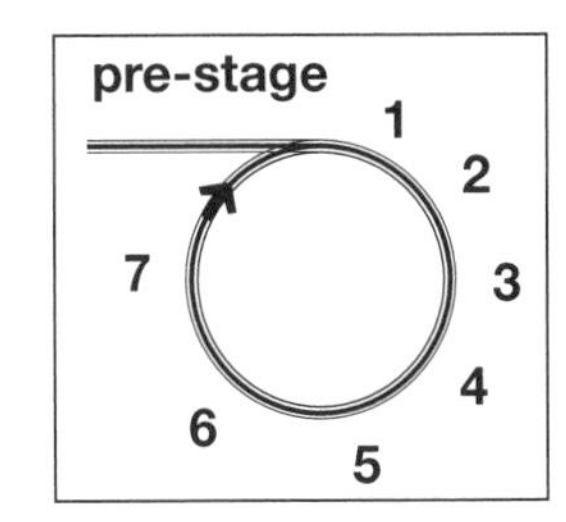

In Section Seven you will learn how ...

- ***you can adapt a unit of work to the Accelerated Learning Cycle***
- ***a Special School teacher combines all of the elements to raise levels of achievement***
- ***four Secondary School teachers apply the model***

The Accelerated Learning Cycle

Pre-Stage
Create the supportive learning environment

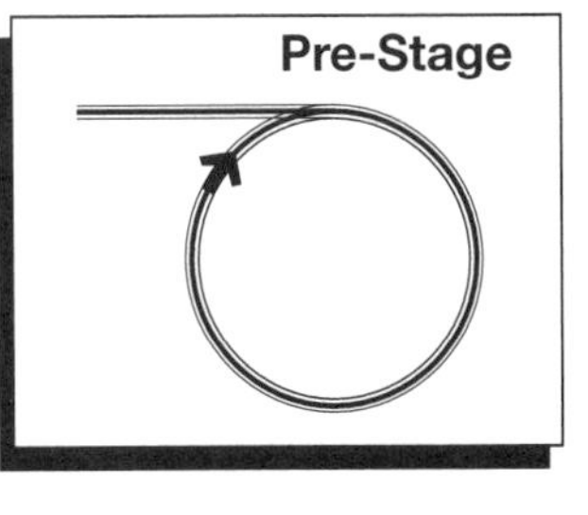

- What strategies are in place to build the self-esteem and self-belief of the learner?
- How do you communicate positive beliefs about success?
- In what ways does your classroom space support learning?
- On entry to your class, how might a learner begin to feel positive about learning?
- What do you know about your learners' preferred learning styles?
- How have you prepared your lessons to accommodate different preferences?

Stage One
Connect the learning

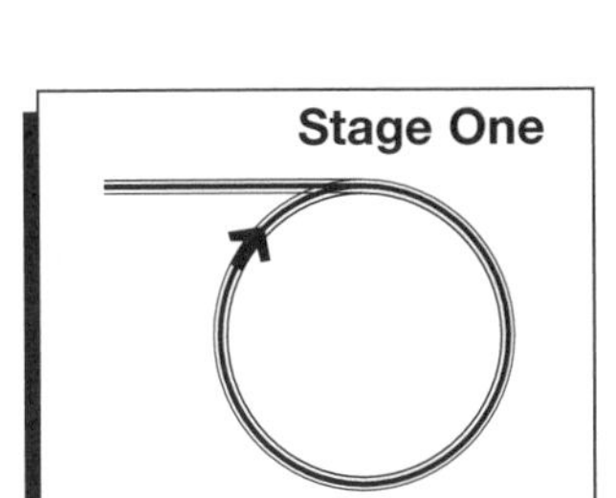

- How would a learner know how this lesson is connected with what went before and what is yet to come?
- Do the learners have long-term goals to help them understand the benefits of this work?
- Do the learners know (if only in outline) the content of the syllabus?
- Is it in 'their' language or recorded appropriately?
- Do the learners know their own preferred learning styles and those of others?
- What knowledge do the learners already have about this topic?
- What strategies do you use to utilize possible prior knowledge?

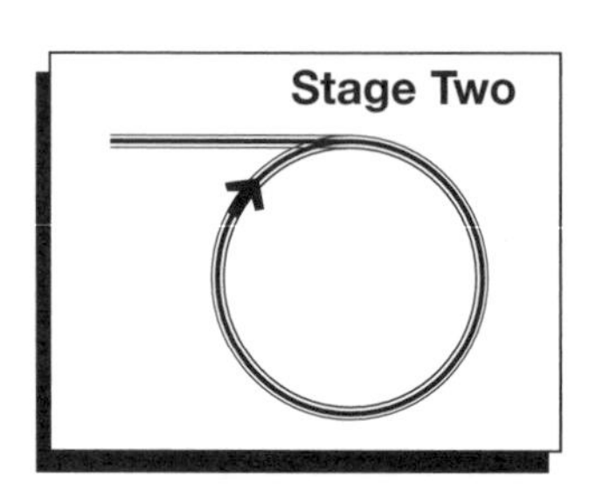

Stage Two
Big Picture

- In what ways can you describe the content of the lesson to access all learners?
- What do you do to alleviate anxiety about the possible difficulty of the content?
- How might the learners record the Big Picture for themselves?
- Can you use the Big Picture as a reference point to record progress?

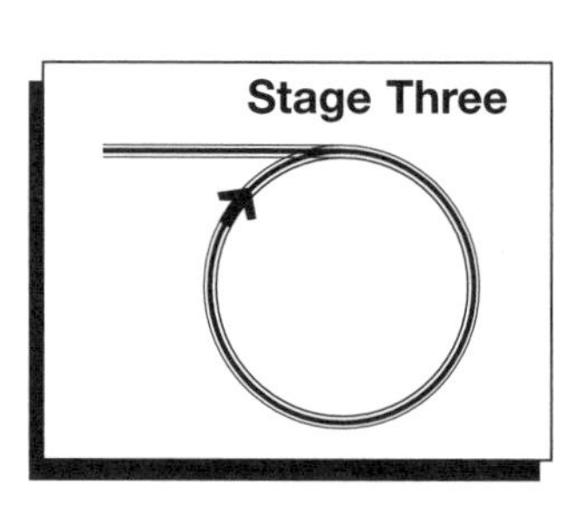

Stage Three
Describe the outcomes

- Can you describe what you hope the learners will have achieved by the end of the lesson?
- Are they able to establish some desired outcomes for themselves?
- How have you broken down the content?
- In what ways have you differentiated?
- Have you anticipated and planned for any extension work or homework?

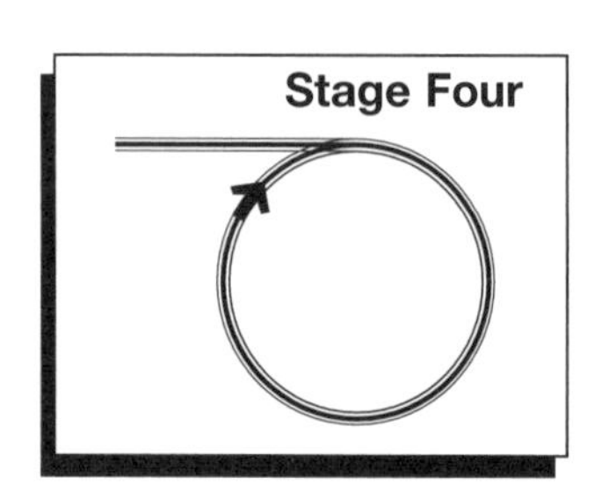

Stage Four
Input

- In what ways can your input include V, A and K?
- Can you utilize other sources of information and input – for example, a guest speaker, video, audio tape?
- Is your input of an appropriate duration?
- Is the language of any auditory tape or text of a visual input at a suitable register or size?
- Is the language multisensory?
- How do you encourage active engagement with your input?
- In what ways might the students find the input memorable!
- How do you check for understanding as you progress?

Stage Five
Activity

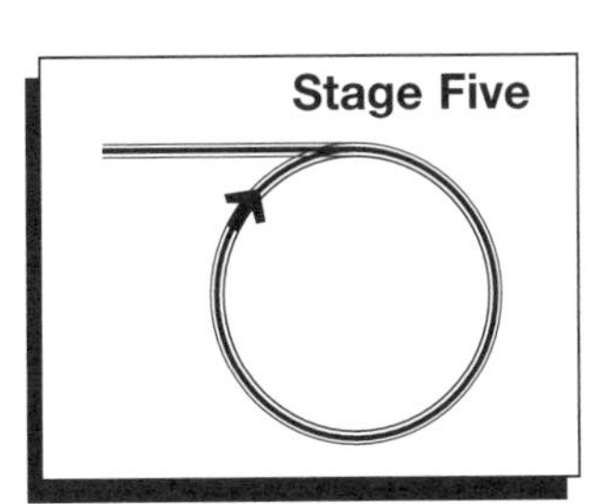

- Which of the seven intelligences does the activity access?
- How might the seven intelligences be balanced over time?
- In what ways are the learners encouraged to make choices?
- Do the participants know and understand the success criteria for the activity?
- Does the activity encourage individual, pair and group work?
- How are the learners encouraged and supported in the activity?
- Can all participants achieve in the activity?

Stage Six
Demonstrate

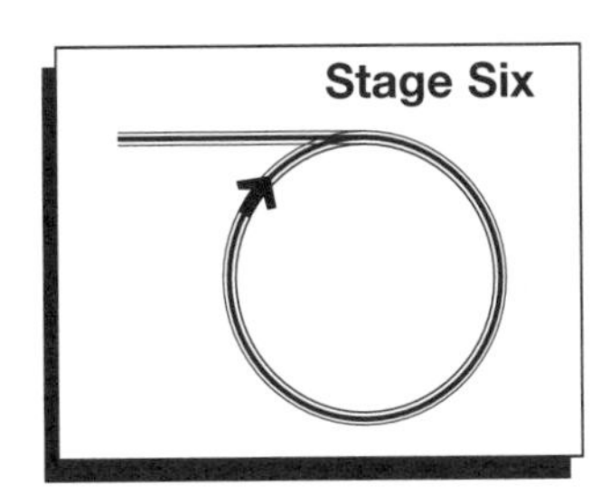

- To whom and at what point will the learners demonstrate their understanding of the new information?
- In what ways can the demonstration be part of the ongoing learning?
- Will the learners have opportunities to reflect on and revise understanding as a result of this stage?
- Is the demonstration differentiated?
- Is it supportive? Is it safe? How might a weaker student be encouraged to take risks?
- How will you assure ultimate success?

Stage Seven
Review for recall and retention

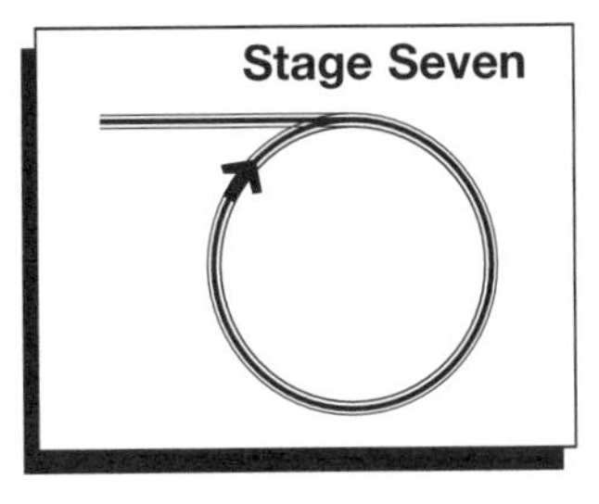

- How often and in what ways do reviews feature in your lessons?
- Are the learners encouraged to self-review or review in pairs or peer groups?
- Against what criteria are reviews conducted?
- How do they encourage long-term recall and understanding?
- At what point do you connect to the goals of the student, the Big Picture and the outcomes for the lesson(s)?

From our own correspondents: case studies from schools

Four of the case studies below are from teachers in Avon schools who, as part of a County of Avon LEA programme to raise pupil motivation and achievement, were participants in a three-day training programme in Accelerated Learning techniques led by the author.

Isobel Clark, Backwell School, Bristol.
Backwell School is an 11–18 mixed Comprehensive School and was recently identified by OFSTED as one of its 203 outstandingly successful schools.

"I'm using a variety of techniques with less able pupils in Years 10 and 11. The Big Picture has been really successful – why didn't I do it before? They work so much better when they can see the route through the work and when they can make choices. Also it disciplines me as a teacher – if I share the Big Picture, I've got to remain within their framework too! We set targets with every piece of work and look at outcomes. I'm beginning to let them set their own outcomes, so the learning outcomes are much more individually tailored.

Raising self-esteem with these youngsters is probably the most important aspect of classroom inter-relations, so I've spent time re-framing negatives into positives and challenging the negative self-talk that says, 'I'm no good at this.' and doing visualizing, 'What will this work look like when you hand it in?' Modelling is useful too. Finding someone in a class who has managed the assignment and done it well – making the process they engaged in clear, so that others can copy. 'So what did it feel like when you sat down to tackle this work? Where were you? How long did you work for? What were you thinking? Seeing? Feeling before you started? What kept you interested?'

I break the work into bite-size chunks and frequently ask the pupils to work with partners to test their knowledge of these chunks. Lots of group improvizations of various scenes from texts helps with the 'Show you know', as does setting quizzes for the other teams and using hot seating.

I try to devise work that uses the seven intelligences but since I only seem to function on two, that's more difficult. However I have succesfully tried:

- writing a rap based on an aspect of a text
- designing a storyboard
- interviewing characters five years on
- writing an additional chapter
- improvizations
- memory maps
- questionnaires
- audio tapes of radio interviews

All these and frequent break-states and Brain Gym® has made a difference in their enthusiasm in the lessons – now it might just be their response to me having more fun or it might be a genuine reaction to an opening up of the process, where it is all now explicit and not implied, I don't know, but it feels good."

Chris Gray, Summerfield Special School, Bath.
Summerfield is an all-age school for pupils with moderate learning difficulties.

Here are the ones (Accelerated Learning techniques) I use:

Years 9 and 10 French language teachers use many of the learning to learn techniques anyway, so I've always used chants, clapping rhythms, memory techniques, music, mimes, physical activities such as throwing juggling balls and circle games, in French. In addition, I now use the Brain Gym® activities for regular 'break-state' times, and do a concert review at the end of each lesson. Pupils enjoy the techniques and find them fun. The sheer ease with which they learn French when it's set in a musical or rhythmic context is astonishing ... so much so that it's easy to forget that this kind of learning needs to be monitored and carefully unpicked to see if it goes deeper than mere recital. The only thing that took a while for pupils to get comfortable with was the concert review, perhaps because classical music always seems to make them laugh anyway! They now expect to have a concert review and are very calm and relaxed during it.

Year 10 PSHE – I use the Brain Gym® activities as warm-ups and break-states, especially the group ones like 'the knot' and moving around throwing the koosh ball in sequence. This seems particularly good for this class, who are prone to quarrels and feuds at break times and often come in to my lessons worked up about things. It has a calming effect, it's fun and it pulls the group together.

My subjects tend to be more skills-based than content-based, so the only context in which I've used memory mapping so far has been a personal one. My son is in his first year at secondary school and has mild literacy problems. He finds it difficult to revise for tests and commit large amounts of factual information to memory in a short time. We now do memory maps, for example, for the formation of rocks in Science ... how does an 11-year-old slowish reader remember words he's never heard of before and has difficulty getting his mind around? He links them to something he has heard of, or to a rhyme, and draws pictures on a memory map. Hence igneous (ignition), metamorphic (Power Rangers – yes, well it apparently meant something to him), basalt (picture of a sheep and a salt cellar), shale (picture of finger on lips and a whale) and so on. This has really made an astonishing difference to his quality of life and to his test marks. Thank you! He also uses concert review.

Roger Gilbert and Ann Manuel, King Edmund Community School, Yate.
King Edmund is an 11–18 mixed comprehensive school in Yate. The school has pupils from a wide variety of social backgrounds.

Roger Gilbert:

Year 9 Science experiment to show the uptake of water in plants using celery sticks and methylene blue dye.

Pupils set up the experiment in groups of 4/5. Their task was to present their findings to the rest of the group in a style of their choosing. Once the experiment was set up the class looked at styles/methods of presenting materials. Activities were based around role play to encourage pupils to better manage their resourcefulness when presenting for example, a round of jousting (a paired competition where their names are said in character and in front of an audience – the more dramatic, extravagant or stylish attracts the most votes). During presentations one group particularly stood out who used the celery stick as a microphone and played out a scene where a reporter interviewed people about the uptake of water in this particular plant and the effect this would have on plant growth.

Year 10 Final Assembly

Music was played on entry to the assembly (*Sultans of Swing* – Dire Straits). After presenting awards to Year 10 students I conducted a 'Concert Review' of the whole year reflecting on the positive experiences and achievements that occurred during the year. I gradually lowered the volume of the music to the point where it was very low and my voice was almost at a whisper, but their attention was fully focused throughout. An amazing experience. ”

Ann Manuel:

Year 11 Business Studies GCSE – Top set

“ Introduced the idea of each person having a preferred style of learning (VAK). Talked very briefly about the different styles. Linked it to the Business Studies lesson by suggesting that there were different strategies that could be used to extract relevant information from text books or information sheets that I usually prepare for the students. I showed the pupils a large example of a memory map on pressure groups. I asked the group to identify the different techniques I had used (highlighting, capital letters, pictures, links to other topics). We then went through the information sheet on pressure groups and I added information that wasn't on the sheet but could be relevant to their mock examination case study. While I was talking I encouraged the pupils to jot down information that wasn't on the sheet. The exercise was then to use the notes and any notes that they had made to draw their own memory map on pressure groups. This took about half an hour, pupils discussing the main points to be used in their memory maps within groups. Follow up was a homework on improving and if necessary redrafting their memory maps. Quote from one of the more sceptical pupils, 'I didn't think this would work, but I went home and tried to remember the main points and when I realized that I could see the map I started to rewrite some history notes in memory maps'. ”

Chris Wardle, Pen Park School, Bristol.
Pen Park is an 11–16 comprehensive school. The school has a high percentage of pupils who receive free school meals. It prides itself on the work it does with its local community. Chris Wardle describes the steps he took after a three-day training course in the techniques of Accelerated Learning.

“ The first step towards using the techniques is to make the commitment to use them. This was helped by the goal-setting ideas we received as part of the training. Some of the techniques were new and did involve extra work at first. However, now they are in place, they are as much a part of my teaching as taking the register. They no longer feel tacked on to my teaching. They are now part of, and indeed direct, my teaching. There are many ways that accelerated learning is included in my lessons. Here are a few.

Reduction of learner stress was one of the areas that I identified as being possible with some of the ideas in accelerated learning. Many of the pupils coming to my classroom are often under stress in some way. This may be because of what happened just before my lesson, in another lesson, or what is happening at home, or indeed because of the thought of my lesson itself. Music can reduce the pupils' stress levels. I also find that it can reduce my own personal stress level, this then gets passed onto the pupils in the way that I teach. A well chosen piece of music from the charts makes the pupils feel a sense of ownership of the culture in the classroom. Music has other advantages: particularly upbeat and energetic music used in the periods before lunch, when blood sugar levels are low, can keep the momentum of the lesson going to the end. If played at a certain volume, music can also reduce the in-class chat when you want it to be at a minimum. I also find that when the music is turned off it take a much shorter time to get the complete attention of the class.

Stress is also reduced if they arrive at my lesson to find that they are immediately involved in a fun Brain Gym® exercise. 'Double Doodle' combined with soothing music is excellent at calming kids after a wet break time. The presentation of the Big Picture can then let the kids know that there is no great ogre of difficulty hiding within the lesson, and if expressed in positive language there is nothing that they think they will not be able to do. Pupils with a low self-image and who feel threatened by their own perceived inabilities at school don't have to be anxious or afraid of the unknown and, therefore, they don't have to opt out. The Big Picture is written on the board using different colours. The purchase of a pack of coloured chalks has changed my board work and, when used with some type of colour coding, has increased the learning that can take place from the chalkboard.

Many of the pupils I teach feel threatened and very unsure of the written word. Knowledge of the different learning styles and intelligences has made me question even more, my use of the written word as an exclusive teaching method in my classroom. Undoubtedly there are times when it is necessary to use the written word but I have certainly started to see a use of the written word as only one way that ideas can be taught. Why restrict yourself to appealing to only a minority of pupils? There are other methods of accessing them. Reading and writing are now only part of my arsenal of teaching methods and not the major methods that they may have been in the past.

I would like to encourage the use of the Concert Review. Drawing the lesson to a close ten minutes early, getting the pupils to pack up, put their coats on, dimming the lights and asking them to relax, possibly by putting their heads down, was at first met with disbelief. But when they realized that I was serious they did as I asked, and then listened while I reviewed the lesson to pulse beat music. When the bell went they were relaxed and listening carefully. Now that they are more used to the procedure, the class can reach that state much more quickly. The pupils seem to enjoy the activity as well as, I hope, taking in the material that is reviewed each time.

Since using the techniques I have found that I have adopted them as my own and have adapted some of the ideas to suit my needs in the classes that I teach. This all follows on from that first step of commitment to using the techniques. ”

Section Eight

Resources and glossary

A selection of useful books

Armstrong, T. — *Seven Kinds of Smart: Identifying and Developing Your Many Intelligences* (Plume, New York, 1993)

Barber, Michael — *The Learning Game – Arguments for an Education Revolution* (Victor Gollancz, London, 1996)

Blum, Deborah — *Sex on the Brain: The Biological Differences between Men and Women* (Penguin, 1997)

Caldwell & Spinks — *The Self-Managing School* (Falmer, 1988)

Campbell, K. — *Teaching and Learning Through Multiple Intelligences* (Allyn and Bacon, 1996)

Carbo, M., Dunn, R. & Dunn, K. — *Teaching Students to Read Through Their Individual Learning Styles* (Prentice Hall, NJ, 1988)

Dennison, P. and Dennison, G.E. — Brain Gym® for Teachers (Edu-Kinesthetics, CA, 1989)

Dhority, Lynn — The ACT Approach: The Use of Suggestion for Integrative Learning (Gordon and Breach, MIT, 1991)

Dilts, R. & Epstein, T. — *Dynamic Learning* (Meta Publications, New York, 1995)

Dryden, G. & Voss, J. — *The Learning Revolution* (Network Educational Press, Stafford, 2001)

Fisher, Robert — *Teaching Children to Learn* (Stanley Thornes, London, 1995)

Fisher, Robert — *Teaching Children to Think* (Blackwell, London, 1991)

Gardner, Howard — *Frames of Mind: The Theory of Multiple Intelligences* (Basic Books, 1993)

Gardner, Howard — *The Unschooled Mind* (Fontana, London, 1993)

Goleman, Daniel — *Emotional Intelligence – Why it Matters More than IQ* (Bloomsbury, 1996)

Greenfield, Susan — *The Human Brain: a guided tour* (Science Masters, 1997)

Hannaford, C. — *Smart Moves: Why Learning Is Not All In Your Head* (Great Ocean Publishers, 1995)

Hart, L. A. — *Human Brain and Human Learning* (Longman, New York, 1983)

Howard, Pierce J. — *The Owner's Manual for the Brain – Everyday Applications from Mind-Brain Research* (Bard Press, Texas, 1994)

James, Oliver — *Britain on the Couch – Treating a Low Serotonin Society* (Century, 1997)

Jensen, Eric — *Brain-Based Learning and Teaching* (Turning Point, 1995)

Jensen, Eric — *Completing the Puzzle: A Brain-Based Approach to Learning* (Turning Point, 1996)

Jensen, Eric — *The Learning Brain* (Turning Point, 1994)

Kovalik, Susan — *Integrated Thematic Instruction: The Model* (SKA, third edition, 1994)

Kotulak, Ronald — *Inside the Brain* (Andrews and McMeel, 1996)

Lazear, D. — *Seven Ways of Teaching: The Artistry of Teaching with Multiple Intelligences* (Zephyr Press, AZ, 1993)

Learning and Teaching Scotland — *Teaching for Effective Learning* (Scottish CCC, 1996)

McCarthy, B. — *The 4MAT System* (Arlington, Excel Publishing, 1982)

Moir A. & Jessell, D. — *Brain Sex: The Real Difference Between Men and Women* (Carol, New York, 1991)

Odam, George — *The Sounding Symbol: Music Education in Action*, (Stanley Thornes, 1995)

Oldroyd & Hall — *Managing Staff Development* (Paul Chapman Publishing, 1991)

Ornstein, Robert — *The Right Mind: Making Sense of the Hemispheres* (Harcourt Brace, New York, 1997)

Perkins, David — *Outsmarting IQ: The Emerging Science of Learnable Intelligence* (The Free Press, New York, 1995)

Rose, Colin & Goll, Louise. — *Accelerate Your Learning* (Accelerated Learning Systems, Aylesbury, 1992)

Rose, Colin & Nicholl Malcolm, J. — *Accelerated Learning for the 21st Century* (Delacorte Press, NY, 1997)

Rosenthal, R., Jacobsen, L. — *Pygmalion in the Classroom* (Holt, Rinehart & Winston, New York, 1968)

Scheele, Paul, R. — *The PhotoReading Whole Mind System* (Learning Strategies Corporation, 1993)

Seligman, M. E. P. — *Learned Optimism* (Knopf, New York, 1991)

Sternberg, R. J. — *Successful Intelligence: How Practical and Creative Intelligence Determine Success in Life* (Plume, New York, 1996)

Wenger, Win — *The Einstein Factor* (Prima, CA, 1996)

Useful contacts

Accelerated Learning in Training and Education, (ALiTE), 45 Wycombe End, Beaconsfield, Bucks HP9 1LZ
(tel: 01494 671444 fax: 01494 671776; email: office@alite.co.uk; www.alite.co.uk)
Training in school and classroom approaches described in this book.

Accelerated Learning Systems Ltd, 50 Aylesbury Road, Aston Clinton, Aylesbury, Bucks, HP22 5AH (tel: 01296 631177; www.accelerated-learning-uk.co.uk
Suppliers of excellent Accelerated Learning publications especially in early years education and in languages.

Anglo-American Books, Crown Buildings, Bancyfelin, Carmarthen, SA33 5ND
(tel: 01267 211880; www.anglo-american.co.uk)
Importers of the most comprehensive selection of books, tapes and videos related to Accelerated Learning, NLP and self-esteem.

Association for Neuro-Linguistic Programming, PO Box 5, Haverfordwest, Wales SA63 4YA (tel: 0870 870 4970; www.anlp.org)
Attracts a membership from business, counselling and education and training. Promotes NLP and related disciplines and produces a quarterly journal called 'Rapport'. NLP training is powerful in work on belief systems and how to change them, utilizing language with precision and outcomes thinking.

The 21st Century Learning Initiative (UK)
Business Centre West, Avenue One, Letchworth, Herts SG6 2HB
(tel: 01462 481107/fax: 01462 481108; www.21learn.org)

The Institute for Transactional Analysis (ITA)
3 Kents Lane, Soham, Ely, Cambs CB7 5DX; www.ita.org.uk

International Alliance for Learning (IAL)
10040 First Street, Encinitas, CA 92024-5059; www.ialearn.org

International Council for Self-Esteem
Contact: Esteem1@aol.com; www.self-esteem-international.org

Network Educational Press Ltd
PO Box 635, Stafford ST16 1BF
(tel: 01785 225515 / fax: 01785 228566; email: enquiries@networkpress.co.uk; www.networkpress.co.uk)

Society for Effective and Affective Learning (SEAL)
37 Park Hall Road, London N2 9PT; www.seal.org.uk

Glossary of terms

Active concert
Summary input of new information by reading over music. The reading is deliberately 'dramatic' and follows the pace and intensity of the music.

Alpha state
A brain wave cycle of 60–70 beats per minute which research has shown is the optimum state for learning. Can be induced through the use of Baroque music.

Anchor
A technique derived from NLP which helps access a desired mental or physical 'state'.

Baroque music
Used in Accelerated Learning for concert review. Baroque music of 60–70 beats per minute induces an Alpha brain wave pattern and helps to access long-term memory.

BASIS
A model for building and maintaining self-esteem and self-belief. BASIS stands for Belonging, Aspirations, Safety, Identity and Success. Successful self-esteem programmes contain all of these elements.

Big Picture
By giving an overview, or Big Picture first, right-brain learners can access the material. Big Picture helps alleviate learner anxiety and helps to connect what is to come with what has gone before.

Brain Gym®
A physical activity which connects left and right brain and is useful for managing the 'state' of learners.

Break-state
In recognizing the optimum time for which a learner at a given development stage can remain on task, 'break-states' help keep the learner in a positive physical and mental state for learning.

CAT scan
Computerized Axial Tomography. A scanning facility which is used to monitor activity in the brain.

Memory map
A non-hierarchical, non-sequential method of taking summary or revision notes. Memory mapping is derived from Tony Buzan's *Mind Map* technique which links left and right brain and which encourages the learner to discern patterns and relationships.

Myelination
The sheathing of the axon to improve the effectiveness of communication between brain cells.

Neuron
Containing cells, axons and dendrites, the neuron is a self-contained communication centre which sends and receives messages.

NLP

Neuro-Linguistic Programming. NLP concerns itself with the difference between competence and excellence in human communication. Sometimes defined as the study of the structure of subjective experience, NLP can be utilized to change unhelpful behaviour patterns and beliefs.

NO LIMIT

An acronym which describes the principles of Accelerated Learning. k**N**ow the brain and how it works. **O**penness and relaxation for optimum learning. **L**earn to capacity. **I**nput through VAK - **V**isual, **A**uditory and **K**inesthetic. **M**ultiple intelligence activities. **I**nvest more through BASIS. **T**ry it, test it and review it.

Passive concert or concert review

A summary review to reinforce learning and improve recall. The content is read to music of 60–70 beats per minute. This engages the brain into an Alpha cycle appropriate for long-term memory.

Peripheral

Any visual stimulus which reinforces positive messages around learning. Peripherals can be a summary of content, keywords, affirmations or role models.

PET scan

Positron Emission Tomography. A scanning facility which is used to monitor activity in the brain.

Positive suggestion

Reinforcement through the learning environment, learning activities and the language and behaviour of the teacher that successful learning will take place and the learner will achieve.

Relative lateralization

The different functions of the two halves of the brain

Sensory language

Language, deliberately chosen, which accesses all representational systems.

Strokes

A unit of attention given or received. Strokes can be positive or negative, conditional or unconditional, real or plastic.

Triune brain

A model of the brain which identifies three distinct functions corresponding to evolutionary stages and which significantly impact on learning.

VAK

Visual, auditory and kinesthetic. Learners, in receiving information through the senses, will have a preferred sensory or representational system. Research suggests 29 per cent of learners will have a visual preference, 34 per cent will be auditory and 37 per cent kinesthetic.

Visualization

A technique for creating or re-creating a scene visually. Visualization can be used to facilitate learning, goal-setting or behavioural changes.

Index